THE STUDENTS' COMPANION

WILFRED D. BEST

CARIBBEAN EDITION

Longman Caribbean

Longman Group UK Limited,
Longman House, Burnt Mill, Harlow,
Essex CM20 2JE, England
and Associated Companies throughout the world

Carlong Publishers Caribbean Limited
PO Box 489,
43 Second Street,
Newport West,
Kingston 10,
Jamaica

Longman Caribbean (Trinidad) Limited,
Boundary Road,
San Juan,
Trinidad

New edition published by
Longman Group UK Ltd 1991
Second impression 1992

Produced by Longman Group (FE) Ltd
Printed in Hong Kong

ISBN 0 582 07518 1

PREFACE

A COMPILATION of this nature could never have been attempted without reference to the work of others. In the preparation of this book I have had to consult constantly numerous encyclopedias, dictionaries, and text-books on a variety of subjects; and I hereby acknowledge my indebtedness to them all.

I wish to record my gratitude to my wife for her unstinted support and encouragement in the preparation of this work. I am extremely grateful for numerous suggestions and complimentary opinions received on the book.

I am also extremely grateful to Mr W. E. Madden former General Manager, U.B.O.T. (now Trinidad and Tobago Oil Company, Trintoc), who did me the honour of "thumbing" through the book with his usual thoroughness.

PREFACE TO THE REVISED EDITION

'The Students' Companion' has been an eminently successful book over the past forty years and is still a great favourite among students, teachers, parents and the general public.

In addition to the International and Caribbean Editions there have been special editions for Nigeria, South East Asia, Zimbabwe, and one for Singapore translated into the native language of that country.

A comprehensive revision of the book has been undertaken at the request of the new publishers, and a new section of selected Choice Quotations has been added to enhance the contents.

I feel confident that the publication of the Revised Version will result in an increase in the popularity of this book.

WILFRED D. BEST

CONTENTS

SINGLE WORDS FOR PHRASES AND SENTENCES

WORDS DENOTING NUMBERS

A number of sheep	flock
A number of whales or porpoises	school, gam
A number of herrings, mackerel etc.	shoal
A number of fish taken in a net	catch, haul
A small number of birds, e.g. partridge	covey
A number of asses	pack
A number of horses, ponies, etc. driven together	drove
A number of cattle or swine feeding or driven together	herd
A number of oxen or horses (two or more) harnessed together	team
A number of birds, bees or insects moving together	flight
A number of peacocks	muster
A number of wolves, hounds or submarines	pack
A number of leopards	leap
A number of geese	gaggle
A number of bees, locusts, ants etc.	swarm
A number of larks or quails or beautiful girls	bevy
A number of bees living in the same place	hive
A number of ants, rabbits or snakes living in the same place	nest
A number of horses kept for riding, racing, breeding	stud
A number of lions, monkeys or cavalry soldiers	troop
A number of rooks	rookery
A colony of seals	rookery

Words denoting numbers (*contd.*)

A number of mules	barren
A number of chickens hatched at the same time	brood
A number of young pigs, dogs, cats brought forth at one birth	litter
A number of kittens	kindle
A collection of fowls, ducks, etc.	poultry
A couple of hawks	cast
A number of wild geese or swans in flight	skein
A collection of wild animals	menagerie, zoo
A number of people at church	congregation
A number of people listening to a concert or lecture	audience
A number of people looking on at a football match, etc.	spectators
A number of people collected together in the street	crowd
A number of people gathered together for some common purpose	gathering, assembly, society
A group of people who get together to work for some cause or common interest	coterie
A number of disorderly people	mob, rabble, canaille
A number of savages	horde
A number of singers in a church	choir
A collection of angels	host
A number of artistes, dancers or acrobats	troupe
A number of actors	company
A number of servants	staff
A number of persons, of the same race, character, etc.	tribe
A number of people following a funeral	cortege
A number of beautiful ladies	bevy
A number of soldiers	army, troop, battalion, regiment
A number of sailors manning a ship	crew
A number of workmen, prisoners, thieves etc.	gang
A collection of slaves	gang, coffle

Words denoting numbers (*contd.*)

A group of constables called to enforce the law	posse
A number of jurymen engaged on a case	jury, panel
A number (more than two) of judges or bishops	bench
A number of directors of a company	board
A collection of poems	anthology
A collection of books	library
A number of pictures, curiosities etc.	collection
A string of pearls	rope
A collection of flowers	bouquet
A collection of flags	bunting
A number of drawers	chest
A number of ships	fleet
A number of merchant ships protected by warships	convoy
A collection of dried plants	herbarium
A number of nuts, grapes on a bunch	cluster
A number of trees	clump
A large collection of trees	forest
A collection of wood, hay, corn, piled together	stack
A cluster of houses in a village	hamlet
A number of stars grouped together	constellation
A collection of rays	pencil
A collection of eggs, a brood of chickens	clutch
A set of furniture, rooms etc.	suite
A quantity of woollen thread	skein
A quantity of bread baked at the same time	batch
A mass of hair	shock, fell
A number of hired applauders, i.e. persons paid to clap	claque
A bundle of hay or straw	truss
A collection of tools	set
A set of bells placed together for a tune to be played on them	carillon

Words denoting numbers (*contd.*)

With these may be added:

A *bale* of cotton, a *bale* of wool, a *tuft* of grass, a *sheaf* of corn, a *sheaf* of arrows, a *hand* of bananas, a *group* of islands, a *crate* of fruit, a *crate* of crockery, a *field* of athletes, a *nest* of machine-guns, a *nest* of shelves.

WORDS DENOTING PLACES

A place where birds are kept	aviary
A place where bees are kept	apiary
A place where fishes are kept	aquarium
A place where rabbits are kept	hutch
A place where rabbits are kept for breeding	warren
A place where pigs are kept	sty
A place for keeping or breeding insects	insectarium
The house or shelter of an Eskimo	igloo
The house or shelter of a Swiss peasant	chalet
The house or shelter of an Arab	dowar
The house or shelter of an American Indian	wigwam, tepee
The house or shelter of a gipsy	caravan
A Zulu village	kraal
The house or shelter of a Kirghis	kabitka
A house or shelter for a dog	kennel
A house or shelter for a horse	stable
A house or shelter for a cow	pen, byre
A house or box in which live pigeons or doves	dovecot
The dwelling-place of an animal underground	burrow
The home of a lion	den
A squirrel's home	drey
A place for fowls to sleep in at nights	roost
The resting place of a wild animal	lair
The house or bed of a hare	form
A nest of a bird of prey	eyrie, aerie
A place where medicines are compounded	dispensary
A place for the treatment of sick people	hospital

Words denoting places (*contd.*)

A place for the care and treatment of convalescents and persons suffering from tuberculosis	sanatorium
A residence for monks or priests	monastery
A residence for nuns	convent
A place where milk is converted into butter and cheese	dairy
A place where bread and cakes are made	bakery
An oven or furnace for baking bricks, pottery, etc.	kiln
A place where animals are slaughtered for the market	abattoir
A factory for manufacturing beer	brewery
A place where spirituous liquors are produced	distillery
A place where crude petroleum is refined	refinery
A place where clothes are washed and ironed	laundry
A place for housing cars	garage
A place for housing aeroplanes	hangar
A place where travellers may obtain lodging and refreshment	hotel, inn
A place where people may obtain food and refreshment	restaurant
A variety show performed in a restaurant	cabaret
The kitchen of a ship	caboose, galley
A house for the residence of students	hostel
A place where books are kept	library
A place where Government records are kept	archives
A place where any manufacture is carried on	factory
A place where scientific experiments are conducted	laboratory
A place where house refuse is reduced to ashes	incinerator
A place where athletic exercises are performed	gymnasium
A place or room for the collection of dried plants	herbarium
A place where treasures of art, curiosities, etc. are preserved or exhibited	museum
A place where articles are deposited for safe-keeping	repository
A place where treasures, stores, ammunition are hidden	cache
A place for storing grain	granary
A place where goods are stored	depot

Words denoting places (*contd.*)

An upper room or storey immediately under the roof	garret
A place where leather is tanned	tannery
A building for the lodging and accommodation of soldiers	barracks
A place where soldiers are quartered	cantonment
A place where money is coined	mint
A place where astronomical observations are taken	observatory
A place where fruit trees are grown	orchard
A place where orphans are housed	orphanage
An institution for the reformation of young offenders	reformatory
A square courtyard bounded by buildings	quadrangle
A wide road lined with trees on both sides	avenue, boulevard
A street open only at one end	cul-de-sac
A Muslim place of worship	mosque
A place where water is collected and stored	reservoir
A place frequented for reasons of pleasure or health	resort
A place with gambling tables, etc.	casino
A nursery where children of poor parents are cared for while their parents are at work	crèche
An enclosure adjoining a race-course where horses are kept before racing	paddock
A covered stall at a fair, horse races, etc.	booth
A place where plates, dishes, pots and other cooking utensils are washed up	scullery
A place where ships are repaired or built	dock
A place where ships are loaded and unloaded	quay
A place for the treatment of the sick in schools	infirmary
The sleeping-rooms in a college or public institution	dormitory
A refreshment hall in monasteries and convents	refectory
A school for infants and young children	kindergarten
A room or building for the preservation of sculpture	glyptotheca
A place where animals are kept alive, and live as nearly as possible as in their natural state	vivarium

Words denoting places (*contd.*)

With these may be grouped the following:

A receptacle for storing coal	bunker, scuttle
A small box in which tea is kept	caddy
A large cask for holding wine or beer	butt, hogshead
A nightclub with no live band of musicians but only recorded music	discotheque
An underground place for storing wine or other provisions	cellar
A portable case for holding papers, drawings, etc.	portfolio
An ornamental glass bottle for holding wine or other alcoholic drinks	decanter
A basket in which a fisherman puts his fish	creel
A lady's handbag or workbag	reticule
A large jug or pitcher for holding water for the washbasin	ewer
A small bottle for holding sauces or condiments for the table	cruet
A case in which the blade of a sword is kept	sheath, scabbard
A large tent used for outdoor functions	marquee

DENOTING PROFESSIONS OR TRADES

One who attends to the diseases of the eye	oculist
One who tests eyesight and sells spectacles	optician
One who attends to sick people and prescribes medicines	physician
One who compounds or sells drugs	druggist, pharmacist
One who treats diseases by performing operations	surgeon
One who attends to the teeth	dentist
One skilled in the care of hands and feet	chiropodist
One who treats diseases by rubbing the muscles	masseur
A physician who assists women at child-birth	obstetrician, accoucheur
A beautician who attends to the hands and fingernails	manicurist
One who drives a motor-car	chauffeur

Denoting professions or trades (*contd.*)

One who manages or attends to an engine	engineer
The person in charge of a ship	captain
The commander of a fleet	admiral
One who carves in stone	sculptor
One who cuts precious stones	lapidary, lapidist
One who writes for the newspapers	journalist, reporter correspondent
One who sets type for books, newspapers etc.	compositor
One who plans and draws the design of buildings and superintends their erection	architect
One who draws plans	draughtsman
One who deals in flowers	florist
One who deals in fruits	fruiterer
One who deals in cattle	drover
One who sells fruits, vegetables, etc., from a barrow	costermonger
One who deals in iron and hardware	ironmonger
One who deals in medicinal herbs	herbalist
One who deals in fish	fishmonger
One who deals in furs	furrier
One who works in brass	brazier
One who sets glass in windows, doors, etc.	glazier
One who deals in wines	vintner
One who works in lead esp. mending water pipes	plumber
One who attends to the fire of a steam engine	stoker
One who makes barrels, tubs, etc.	cooper
One employed as a labourer to do excavating work	navvy
One who makes and sells ladies' hats	milliner
One who sells small articles such as ribbons, laces, thread	haberdasher
One who deals in cloths and other fabrics	draper
One who deals in silks, cotton, woollen, and linen goods	mercer
A professional rider in horse races	jockey
One who shoes horses	farrier

Denoting professions or trades (*contd.*)

One who looks after horses at an inn	ostler, hostler
One who studies rocks and soils	geologist
One who studies the past through objects left behind	archaeologist
One who studies the stars	astronomer
One who foretells things by the stars	astrologer
One who flies an aeroplane	pilot, aviator
One who works in a coal-mine	collier
A Japanese girl who entertains by singing and dancing	geisha
One who converts raw hide into leather	tanner
One who makes or deals in cutting instruments, e.g. knives	cutler
One who cleans the street	scavenger
A woman employed to clean inside buildings	charwoman
One who sells sweets and pastries	confectioner
One who induces or entraps men to serve in the army or navy	crimp
One who collects the bets and pays out to the winner in a gambling club	croupier
One who takes care of a building	janitor
One who sells fowls, ducks, turkeys, etc.	poulterer
One who pays out money at a bank	cashier, teller
One who makes and sells cushions and covers chairs, motor-car seats etc.	upholsterer
One who lends money at exorbitant interest	usurer
One who draws maps	cartographer
One who collects postage stamps	philatelist
One who performs tricks by sleight of hand	conjuror prestidigitator, juggler
One who walks on ropes	funambulist
One who performs daring gymnastic feats	acrobat
One who pastures cattle for the market	grazier
One who travels from place to place selling miscellaneous articles	huckster, pedlar, chapman, hawker

Denoting professions or trades (*contd.*)

One who makes pots, cups, etc.	potter
One who goes from place to place mending pots, pans etc.	tinker
One who mends shoes	shoemaker, cobbler
One who travels from place to place selling religious articles	colporteur
A teacher who travels from place to place to give instruction	peripatetic
One who watches over students taking an examination	invigilator
A person in charge of a museum	curator
One who is in charge of giving assistance to the poor; a hospital welfare officer	almoner
The person in charge of a library	librarian
The head of a college	principal
The head of a town council or corporation	Mayor
One who lends money and keeps goods as security	pawnbroker
One who draws up contracts and also lends money on interest	scrivener
One who builds ships	shipwright
One who loads and unloads ships	stevedore
One who makes wheels for carriages and carts	wheelwright
One who sells articles at public sales	auctioneer
A tradesman who manages funerals	mortician, undertaker
One skilled in the treatment of diseases of animals	veterinarian
One who writes shorthand	stenographer
One who writes poetry	poet
One who write novels	novelist
One who writes books	author
One who compiles a dictionary	lexicographer
One who sells paper, ink, pens and writing materials	stationer
One who preserves the skins of animals and mounts them so as to resemble the living animals	taxidermist
One versed in the science of human races, their varieties and origin	ethnologist

Denoting professions or trades (*contd.*)

One who studies the evolution of mankind	anthropologist
One who studies the working of the human mind	psychologist
One who makes or sells candles	chandler
One who works or deals in feathers for apparel	plumassier
The treasurer of a college or university	bursar
An officer in charge of the stores, provisions and accounts on a ship	purser

NAMES BY WHICH PERSONS WITH CERTAIN CHARACTERISTICS ARE KNOWN

One who looks on the bright side of things	optimist
One who looks on the dark side of things	pessimist
One who devotes his service or wealth for the love of mankind	philanthropist
A hater of mankind	misanthrope, misanthropist
One who becomes the favourite of a distinguished personage and serves him as a slave	minion
One who sneers at the aims and beliefs of his fellow men	cynic
One who walks in his sleep	somnambulist
One who talks in his sleep	somniloquist
One who has the art of speaking in such a way that the sound seems to come from another person	ventriloquist
One who delights to speak about himself or thinks only of his own welfare	egotist
One who devotes his life to the welfare and interests of other people	altruist
One who runs away from justice or the law	fugitive
One who takes refuge in a foreign country	refugee, alien
One who is banished from his home or his country	exile
One who maliciously sets fire to a building	incendiary
One who has an irresistible tendency to steal	kleptomaniac
One who steals books	biblioklept
One who dies for a noble cause	martyr
One who retires from society to live a solitary life	recluse, hermit

Names by which persons with certain characteristics are known (*contd.*)

One who offers his service of his own free will	volunteer
One who is compelled by law to serve as a soldier	conscript
A soldier or a sailor newly enlisted	recruit
One new to anything	novice, tyro, neophyte
A lover of animals	zoophilist
One who is withdrawn and has little interest in things besides self	introvert
One who is outward-looking, exuberant, and has wide interests	extrovert
One who engages in an occupation for gain, e.g. sport	professional
One who engages in any pursuit for the love of it, and not for gain	amateur
One who starts a new business or enterprise	entrepreneur
One who feeds on fruits	fruitarian
One who eats no animal flesh	vegetarian
One who feeds on human flesh	cannibal
One who journeys from place to place	itinerant
One who journeys on foot	pedestrian
One who journeys to a holy place	pilgrim
One who goes from place to place begging alms	mendicant, beggar
A leader of the people who can sway his followers by his oratory	demagogue
One whose reasoning is clever yet false	sophist
One who makes a display of his learning	pedant
One who has special skill in judging art, music, tastes, etc.	connoisseur
An expert at story-telling	raconteur
One who listens to the conversation of others	eavesdropper
One who loves his country and serves it devotedly	patriot

Names by which persons with certain characteristics are known (*contd.*)

One who foretells events	prophet
One devoted to the pleasures of eating and drinking	epicure
One given up to luxurious living	sybarite
One given to sensual pleasures and bodily enjoyment	voluptuary
One who pretends to be what he is not	hypocrite, impostor
One who pretends to know a great deal about everything	mountebank, charlatan, quack
One who imitates the voice, gestures etc. of another	mimic
One who can enable people speaking different languages to understand each other	interpreter
One versed in many languages	linguist
One who can use both hands with equal facility	ambidexter
A person sixty years old	sexagenarian
A person seventy years old	septuagenarian
A person eighty years old	octogenarian
A person ninety years old	nonagenarian
A person one hundred years old	centenarian
A model of a human figure for displaying clothing	mannequin
One who entertains another	host, hostess
One who accompanies a young lady to public places	chaperon
One under the protection of another	protégé, ward
One who searches for minerals or mining sites	prospector
A messenger sent in great haste	courier
One who steers a boat	coxswain
An acrobat who bends his body into various shapes	contortionist
A hater of marriage	misogamist
A hater of women	misogynist
A person in a low state of health, or over-anxious about his health	valetudinarian
One who worries a candidate for election by interruption and awkward questions	heckler
One who tries to get votes for an election candidate	canvasser

Names by which persons with certain characteristics are known (*contd.*)

An authority on pronunciation	orthoepist
An unthankful person	ingrate
One sent out on a mission	emissary
A person who collects things belonging to ancient times	antiquary
One who collects coins	numismatist
One who has been before another in office or employment	predecessor
One who takes over after another in office or employment	successor
One who kills political figures	assassin
A partner in crime	accomplice
One who works along with another	coadjutor
One living at the same time as another	contemporary
One who is opposed to intellectual progress	obscurant
One who eats all kinds of food	pantophagist
One who has an irresistable desire for alcoholic drinks	dipsomaniac, alcoholic
One who abstains from alcoholic drinks	teetotaller
A diplomat of the highest rank who represents his government in another country	ambassador
A diplomat of lower rank than an ambassador	chargé d'affaires
A woman with light-coloured hair	blonde
A woman with dark hair	brunette
A person who dresses up women's hair	hairdresser, coiffeur
A noisy, abusive, scolding woman	termagant
A young lady who is making her first appearance at a public dance, or being presented at Court	debutante
One who hides away on a ship to obtain a free passage	stowaway
One who shoots with bows and arrows	archer
One who fishes with a rod	angler
One employed to lead another into a trap	decoy

PERTAINING TO GOVERNMENT

Government of the people, for the people and by the people	democracy
Government by a sovereign with uncontrolled authority	autocracy, despotism
Government by the nobility	aristocracy
Government by departments of state	bureaucracy
Government by a few	oligarchy
Government by the wealthy	plutocracy
Government by priests or ecclesiastics	hierarchy, hagiarchy, hagiocracy
Government by divine guidance	theocracy
Government of the church by bishops	episcopacy
Government by a military class	statocracy
Government by the worst citizens	kakistocracy
The right of self-government	autonomy
The science of government	politics
A radical change in government	revolution
To decide a political question by the direct vote of the whole electorate	referendum
The period between two reigns	interregnum
An officer appointed by the government to receive and investigate grievances of its citizens against the administration	ombudsman
A general pardon by a government to a certain class of offenders	amnesty
One who governs a kingdom during the infancy, absence, or disability of the sovereign	regent
The wife or husband of a king or queen	consort
An official numbering of the population	census
Facts and figures	statistics

WORDS PERTAINING TO THE CHURCH

The district under the jurisdiction of a bishop	diocese
The principal church in the diocese	cathedral
A passage between the pews in a church	aisle
One who has charge of a church building	sexton
One who leads people to their seats in a church	verger
The money given by the congregation at a church service	offertory
The ceremony at which a man becomes a priest	ordination
A chapel or vault beneath a church usually used for the burial of the dead	crypt
A letter from the Pope to all Roman Catholics	encyclical
A room attached to the church in which vestments are kept and in which church officials meet	vestry
The residence of a priest or minister or vicar	presbytery, manse, vicarage, rectory
One who sings in the choir	chorister
A reading-desk from which the scriptures are read	lectern
The stand from which a preacher delivers his sermon	pulpit
A bishop's staff	crosier
A bishop's cap or headdress	mitre
The garments of parsons and choristers	vestments
A long loose gown worn by priests and choristers	cassock
The cassock of a Roman Catholic priest	soutane
A loose white vestment worn over the cassock	surplice
A vestment like a surplice worn by bishops	rochet
A cloak-like vestment worn by priests at processions or solemn ceremonies	cope
In Roman Catholic churches a vessel in which the consecrated host is presented for adoration	monstrance
The cup used in the Eucharist	chalice
The priest officiating at the Holy Communion	celebrant

Words pertaining to the Church (*contd.*)

A rich covering carried over a priest in procession	canopy
The body of ministers ordained for the work in the Christian church	clergy
The people, as distinct from the clergy	laity
A council of clergymen	synod
The vessel or basin containing water for baptism	font
The head of a cathedral	dean
A clergyman next in rank after a bishop	archdeacon
One in the lowest degree of holy orders in the Anglican Church	deacon
A clergyman assigned to a regiment, a warship, prison or public institution	chaplain
The circle of light seen in pictures around the head of Jesus Christ, the Virgin Mary, and the Saints	halo, aureole
One who goes to heathen countries to spread the Gospel of Christ	missionary
Morning service of the Anglican Church	matins
Evening service	vespers, evensong
A hymn of praise to the Holy Trinity	doxology
One who does not believe in the existence of God	atheist
One who believes that man can have no knowledge of God but only of natural phenomena	agnostic
One who renounces his religious vows or foresakes his religious principles	apostate
One who is converted from one religion to another	proselyte
One who believes in a single God	monotheist
One who believes in many Gods	polytheist
One intolerantly devoted to a particular creed	bigot
To utter profane language against God or anything holy	blaspheme
Holding opinions contrary to the true doctrine of the church so as to cause a division	heresy
Violating or profaning religious things	sacrilege

Words pertaining to the Church (*Contd.*)

A breaker of church images or ornaments	iconoclast
The central or main part of a church	nave
The eastern end of a church	chancel
A portion of a large church or public institution set apart with an altar of its own where services can be held for a small number of people	chapel
One who assists at services by lighting candles etc.	acolyte
A vessel for burning incense	censer
The salary of a clergyman	stipend
Method of administering Holy Communion by dipping the bread into the wine and offering both at once	intinction
The land furnishing part of the church revenue	glebe

PERTAINING TO MARRIAGE

One who has only one wife or husband at a time	monogamist
The practice of having more than one husband or wife at the same time	polygamy
One who marries a second wife or husband while the legal spouse is alive	bigamist
Man who has more than one wife at a time	polygynist
Woman who has more than one husband at a time	polyandrist
A hater of marriage	misogamist
One vowed to a single or unmarried life	celibate
Legal dissolution of the marriage of husband and wife	divorce
Payment of money allowed to a wife on legal separation from her husband	alimony
A man whose wife is dead	widower
A woman whose husband is dead	widow
The property which a new wife brings to her husband	dowry
One engaged to be married	fiancé, fiancée
Engaged to be married	betrothed, affianced
A bride's outfit	trousseau
Proclamation of intended marriage	banns
To run away with a lover in order to get married secretly	elope

SCIENCES AND ARTS

An institution for education in the arts and sciences	polytechnic
The study of all heavenly bodies and the earth in relation to them	astronomy
The art of tilling the soil	agriculture
The art of cultivating and managing gardens	horticulture
The science of land management	agronomics
The science of family descent	genealogy
The study of ancient buildings and prehistoric remains	archaeology
The study of ancient writings	palaeography
The art of beautiful hand-writing	calligraphy
The art of making maps and charts	cartography
The art of metal-working	metallurgy
The study of coins	numismatics
The science of numbers	mathematics
The science of measuring	mensuration
The art of measuring land	surveying
The science of triangles	trigonometry
The art of preserving skins	taxidermy
The art of making fireworks	pyrotechnics
The science of colours	chromatics
The art of elegant speech or writing	rhetoric
The art of effective speaking or oral reading	elocution
The art of telling the future by the study of the stars	astrology
The study of mankind	anthropology
The science which deals with the varieties of the human race	ethnology
The science of the structure of the human body	anatomy
The science which deals with the way in which the human body works	physiology
The scientific study of industrial arts	technology
The study of the human mind	psychology

Sciences and Arts (*contd.*)

The study of the human face	physiognomy
The study of physical life or living matter	biology
The study of plants	botany
The natural history of animals	zoology
The study of rocks and soils	geology
The study of birds	ornithology
The study of eggs	oology
The study of mountains	orology
The study of languages	philology
The study of the origin and history of words	etymology
The study of stars	astronomy
The study of lakes or of pond life	limnology

MEDICAL

A disease affecting many persons at the same place and time	epidemic
A disease widely epidemic	pandemic
A disease confined to a particular district or place	endemic
A disease affecting widely scattered groups of people	sporadic
A substance which destroys or weakens germs	antiseptic
A substance used by dentists to deaden the gum and nerve	cocaine
A substance used in surgery to produce unconsciousness	chloroform
Any medicine which produces insensibility	anaesthetic
A medicine which alleviates pain	analgesic, anodyne
The mark or scar left after a wound is healed	cicatrice, cicatrix
A powder or paste (usually sweet-smelling) used for cleaning the teeth	toothpaste, dentrifrice
A medicine to counteract poison	antidote
An instrument used by physicians for listening to the action of the heart and lungs	stethoscope
Free or exempt from infection	immune

Medical (*contd.*)

Bad, foul-smelling breath	halitosis
To place apart to prevent from infecting others	isolate
A medicine for producing sleep	narcotic, opiate
A medicine to cause vomiting	emetic
Confinement to one place to avoid spread of infection	quarantine
To cut off a part of a person's body which is infected	amputate
A cure for all diseases	panacea
One who is recovering from illness	convalescent
Gradual recovery from illness	convalescence
A vehicle for conveying sick or injured people to the hospital	ambulance
Want or poorness of blood	anaemia
Affecting the lungs	pulmonary
A substance to keep down evil smells	deodorant
To be able to tell the nature of a disease by its symptoms	diagnose
A forecast of the result of a disease or illness	prognosis
To disinfect by smoke	fumigate
The science of diseases of the human body	pathology
The mosquito which transmits filaria	culex
The mosquito which transmits malaria	anopheles
The mosquito which transmits yellow fever	stegomyia

DEATH

Fainting or death due to being deprived of air	asphyxia
The dead body of a human being	corpse
The dead body of an animal	carcass
Dead and decaying flesh (esp. of animals)	carrion
A place where dead bodies are temporarily placed	mortuary
A place where the bodies of persons found dead are placed for identification	morgue
Disposal of a dead body by burning	cremation
To preserve a dead body from putrefaction	embalm
The cloth which is wrapped round a dead body	winding-sheet

Death (*contd.*)

To dig up a corpse	exhume
A frame on which a dead body is conveyed	bier
A pile of wood on which a dead body is burned	pyre
A vehicle for taking dead bodies to the cemetary	hearse
A place where dead bodies are interred	cemetery
An examination of a dead body	post-mortem, autopsy
Occurring after death	posthumous
An inscription on a tomb	epitaph
A vault beneath a church used for burial	crypt
A stone coffin, especially one made of limestone	sarcophagus
Underground caves with burying places for the dead	catacombs
A very expensive and elaborately built tomb	mausoleum
The practice of putting painlessly to death	euthanasia
An account in the newspaper of the funeral of one deceased	obituary
To die, without leaving a will	intestate
The property left to someone by a will	legacy
Mass for the dead	requiem
The act of killing oneself	suicide
The act of killing a human being	homicide
Murder of a new-born child	infanticide
Murder of a brother	fratricide
Murder of a sister	sororicide
Murder of a mother	matricide
Murder of a father	patricide
Murder of a parent	parricide
Murder of a king	regicide
Rising from the dead	resurrection
A monument set up for persons who are buried elsewhere	cenotaph
Killed by an electric current	electrocuted

WORDS CONNECTED WITH NATURE STUDY

At home equally on land or in water	amphibious
Living or going in flocks or herds	gregarious
The dormant condition in which plants and animals pass the winter	hibernation
(Trees) which lose their leaves annually	deciduous
A cud-chewing animal, e.g. the cow	ruminant
A gnawing animal, e.g. the rat	rodent
A four-footed animal	quadruped
Animals which carry their young in a pouch, e.g. kangaroo	marsupials
Soil composed largely of decayed vegetable matter	humus
Soil washed down and carried away by rivers	alluvium
A preparation for killing insects	insecticide
A plant or animal growing on another	parasite
Lasting for a single year or season	annual
Lasting for two years	biennial
Living for many years	perennial
That part of the seed which develops into the plant	embryo, germ
The part of the embryo which forms the root	radicle
The part of the embryo which forms the stem	plumule
The process by which the young plant begins to grow	germination
The process by which plants give off excess water through their leaves	transpiration
The process by which plants manufacture food	assimilation
The process by means of which plants and animals breathe	respiration
The process by which plants take up mineral salts in solution through their roots	absorption
Tiny openings on the under-surface of leaves through which the plant breathes	stomata
The green colouring matter in the leaves of plants	chlorophyll
A slimy substance between the wood and bark of a stem	cambium

Words connected with nature study (*contd.*)

Two leaf-like appendages at the base of some leaves	stipules
A spiral shoot of a plant which winds itself round another body for support	tendril
The process by which pollen dust is transferred from the stamen to the pistil	pollination
The entrance of the pollen grains into the ovules in the ovary	fertilisation
An instrument for making holes in the soil for seeds or seedlings	dibble
One who studies plant and animal life	naturalist
The parts of an animal killed for food which are rejected or considered waste	offal
Rock from which metal is extracted	ore
The track of a wild animal	spoor
The meat of deer	venison
The flesh of sheep	mutton
A cluster of flowers on a branch	inflorescence
The seed-leaves of the embryo	cotyledon
Plants with one seed-leaf, e.g. corn	mono-cotyledonous
Plants with two seed-leaves, e.g. lime	di-cotyledonous
A thick underground stem	rhizome
Animals with backbone	vertebrates
Animals without backbone	invertebrates
The inside of a nut	kernel
The central or innermost part of a fruit	core
The animals of a certain region	fauna
The plants and vegetation of a certain region	flora
The last stage through which an insect passes before it becomes a perfect insect	chrysalis
Absence of rain for a long time	drought
A flower garden with walks of grass or gravel separating the beds	parterre
To supply land with water by artificial means	irrigate

Words connected with nature study (*contd.*)

The feelers of an insect	antennae
The dead skin cast off by a snake	slough

OPPOSITES

Writing that is easy to read	legible
Writing that is difficult to decipher	illegible
Able to read	literate
Unable to read	illiterate
Fit for food	edible
Unfit for human consumption	inedible
Fit to be chosen or selected	eligible
Not having the qualities of being chosen	ineligible
Loud enough to be heard	audible
Not distinct enough to be heard	inaudible
Born of married parents	legitimate
Born of unmarried parents	illegitimate

With these may be grouped the following:

To move from one country to another	migrate
One who leaves his country to settle in another	emigrant
One who comes into a foreign country to settle there	immigrant
To send back a person to his own country	repatriate
To banish from one's country	expatriate
Love of one's country	patriotism
Goods brought into a country	imports
Goods carried out of a country	exports
A list or table of duties payable on exports or imports	tariff
A list of goods despatched with quantity and price to the purchaser	invoice
One to whom goods are despatched	consignee
The highest point of anything	zenith
The lowest point of anything	nadir

Opposites (*contd.*)

The beginning or first	alpha
The last or end	omega

NEGATIVES

That which cannot be pierced or penetrated	impenetrable
That which cannot be taken by assault	impregnable
That which cannot be passed	impassable
That which cannot be conquered	invincible
That which cannot be wounded or injured	invulnerable
That which cannot be lessened	irreducible
That which cannot be repaired or remedied	irreparable
That which cannot be made good in case of loss	irreplaceable
That which cannot be imitated	inimitable
That which cannot be rubbed out or blotted out	ineffaceable, indelible
Incapable of making errors	infallible
Incapable of being destroyed	indestructible
Incapable of being redeemed from evil, i.e. beyond correction	incorrigible
Incapable of being burnt	incombustible
That which cannot be avoided or prevented	inevitable
That which cannot be made plain or understood	inexplicable
Enduring for all times	imperishable
Not admitting the passage or entrances of water etc.	impervious
Not endowed with animal life	inanimate
Absolutely necessary, cannot be dispensed with	indispensable
Not to the point	irrelevant
Unable to die	immortal
That which cannot be moved	immovable
That which cannot be heard	inaudible
That which cannot be seen	invisible

SCIENTIFIC INSTRUMENTS

An instrument for measuring altitudes	altimeter
An instrument used for measuring heat or cold	thermometer
An instrument for measuring the pressure of the air	barometer
An instrument for measuring the force or variation of the wind	anemometer
An instrument for making very small objects appear large	microscope
An instrument for seeing distant objects	telescope
An instrument for transmitting the voice to a distance	telephone
An instrument for increasing the volume of the voice	microphone
An instrument for enabling persons inside a submarine to see objects above the surface of the water	periscope
An instrument for detecting earthquakes	seismograph
An instrument for taking photographs	camera
An instrument for measuring the speed of a motor-car	speedometer
An instrument for beating time during a musical performance	metronome
An instrument for measuring minute distances	micrometer
An instrument for measuring gases	manometer
An instrument for distinguishing precious stones	lithoscope
An instrument for recording revolutions	gyrograph
An instrument for measuring electric current	ammeter
An instrument which when put to both eyes enables a person to see distant objects as if they were near	binoculars
A calculator with sliding counters used especially by the Chinese people	abacus

MILITARY WORDS

An unprovoked attack by an enemy	aggression
Nations carrying on warfare	belligerents
Compulsory enrolment as soldiers or sailors	conscription

Military words (*contd.*)

The killed or wounded in battle	casualties
An officer who assists his commanding officer to carry out administrative duties	adjutant
A number of ships travelling together under escort for the sake of safety	convoy
Smuggling of goods or engaging in prohibited traffic	contraband
The act or practice of spying	espionage
To remove from one place to another to avoid the destruction of war	evacuate
An order prohibiting ships to leave the ports	embargo
To make troops, ships etc. ready for war service	mobilise
To enter a country as an enemy	invade
Taking neither side in the struggle, that is, not assisting either of the belligerents	neutral
A foreigner in a belligerent country	alien
To keep citizens in confinement	intern
Shells, bombs, military stores	ammunition
Heavy guns, artillery and army stores	ordnance
A knife fixed on to the end of a gun	bayonet
A promise given by a prisoner not to try to escape if given temporary release	parole
Long strips of cloth bound round the legs of a soldier from the ankle to the knee	puttees
Music for awakening soldiers in the morning	reveille
A place where naval or military weapons are made or stored	armoury, arsenal
An apparatus which opens like an umbrella to enable a person to drop safely from an aircraft	parachute
A shower of bullets	volley
The firing of many guns at the same time to mark an occasion	salvo
Horse-soldiers	cavalry
Foot-soldiers	infantry
A number of firearms being discharged continuously	fusillade

Military words (*contd.*)

To make an examination or preliminary survey of enemy territory or military objective	reconnoitre
An agreement to stop fighting	armistice
To surrender to an enemy on agreed terms	capitulate
To reduce to nothing	annihilate
A general pardon of offenders	amnesty
The main division of an army	battalion
To surround a place with the intention of capturing it	besiege
A soldier recently enlisted for service	recruit
A soldier's holiday	leave, furlough
Official reports on the progress of the war	bulletin
The art of conducting negotiations between nations	diplomacy
A body of soldiers stationed in a fortress to defend it	garrison
A fortified place defended by soldiers, cannons, etc.	garrison
A broad belt worn across the shoulder and chest, with pockets for carrying ammunition	bandolier
A person who is forced by law to become a soldier	conscript
An irregular warfare conducted by scattered or independent bands	guerilla war
Movement of ships or troops in order to secure an advantage over the enemy	manoeuvre
To seize for military use	commandeer
To release from the army	demobilise
An encampment in the open air	bivouac
To camp in the open air without tents or covering	bivouac
A place where soldiers can buy drinks and other refreshments	canteen

LITERARY

A book in which the events of each day are recorded	diary
A book containing the words of a language with their definitions, in alphabetical order	dictionary
A book of names and addresses	directory

Literary (*contd.*)

A book of accounts showing debits and credits	ledger
Word for word	verbatim
The sum of all the words which may be used by a particular person	vocabulary
The ordinary, everyday language of a people	vernacular
A book containing information on all branches of knowledge	encyclopedia
A book with blank pages for putting autographs, pictures, stamps, etc.	album
A list of books in a library	catalogue, bibliography
A list of explanations of rare, technical or obsolete words	glossary
A written account, usually in book form, of the interesting and memorable experiences of one's life	memoirs
The trade mark of the maker seen on paper when it is held up to the light	watermark
One who pretends to have a great deal of knowledge	wiseacre
A brief summary of a book	epitome
A collection of choice poems or literary extracts	anthology
An extract or selection from a book of writing	excerpt
The heading or short description of a newspaper article, chapter of a book etc.	caption
A statement which is accepted as true without proof	axiom
A list of the headings of the business to be transacted at a meeting	agenda
Language which is confused and unintelligible	jargon
A declaration of plans and promises put forward by a candidate for election, a political party or a sovereign	manifesto
To remove the offensive portions of a book	expurgate
Still in use (of books published long ago)	extant
A picture facing the title of a book	frontispiece
The exclusive right of an author or his heirs to publish or sell copies of his writings	copyright
An error or misprint in printing, or writing	erratum
An exact copy of handwriting, printing, or of a picture	facsimile

Literary (*contd.*)

A principle or standard by which anything is, or can be judged	criterion
Delivered (of a speech) without previous preparation	extempore, impromptu
A short speech by a player at the beginning of a play	prologue
An excess of words	verbiage
Beautiful handwriting	calligraphy
Bad handwriting or spelling	cacography
A short speech by a player at the end of a play	epilogue
Passing off another author's work as one's own	plagiarism
A writing or speech in praise of a person	eulogy, encomium
A person's own handwriting	autograph
A record of one's life written by himself	autobiography
The history of the life of a person	biography
A humorous play, having a happy ending	comedy
A play with a sad or tragic end	tragedy
A mournful song (or poem) for the dead	dirge
A poem of lamentation, especially for the dead	elegy
A conversation between two persons	dialogue
Speaking to oneself	soliloquy
Study by night	lucubration
A succession of the same initial letters in a passage	alliteration
A note to help the memory	memorandum
A list of articles and their description	inventory
The concluding part of a speech	peroration
A noisy or vehement speech intended to excite passions	harangue
To make expressive gestures or motions while speaking	gesticulate
Language that is very much used	hackneyed
To pronounce words distinctly	enunciate
One who writes plays	dramatist, playwright
A poem in which the first letters of each line, taken in order, form a name or a sentence	acrostic

WORDS PERTAINING TO COOKING

To roast beef, pork or chicken dipped in sauce over an open fire	barbecue
To moisten meat or fish with butter or fat during cooking	baste
A rich thick soup made from meat or fish	bisque
To cook meat until brown and then allow to simmer in a covered pan	braise
A soup made with fish, meat or vegetables	broth
Small pieces of buttered toast served with a paste of cheese, fish or meat	canapés
A pyrex dish in which food is baked and served	casserole
A dish made from fish or pork stewed with vegetables, often in milk	chowder
A condiment of East Indian origin made from green mangoes, pepper, onions, curry powder, etc	chutney
A kitchen utensil with small holes at the bottom and sides for draining	colander
A salad made from shredded raw cabbage, carrots, sweet peppers in mayonnaise sauce	coleslaw
A clear soup made of meat and vegetables	consommé
A thin slice of meat for frying or broiling	cutlet
Flour moistened with water or milk for baking bread or pastry	dough
A slice of fish removed from the bone	filet
A dish of meat cut into small pieces, fried or stewed and served with gravy	fricassee
A stew made with beef or veal and vegetables seasoned with mild red pepper (paprika)	goulash
A stew of meat, especially mutton, and vegetables	haricot
A dish of chopped meat and potatoes, sautéd, baked or browned	hash
An appetiser consisting of olives, asparagus and other savouries served before the main meal	hors d'oeuvre

Words pertaining to cooking (*contd.*)

A dish of rice, fish, bacon, onions, etc	kedgeree
A mixture of seasoning in which fish or meat is soaked before cooking	marinade
A thick soup of Italian origin made with vegetables and meat stock	minestrone
Vegetables or meat boiled to a thick soup and then strained	puree
A dish of rice, meat, onions and butter cooked in broth and served instead of a soup	risotto
To fry quickly in a little oil or fat	sauté
To keep a pot on low fire to bring out the flavour in food	simmer
The broth from boiled meat, fish or bones used as a foundation for preparing soup	stock

MISCELLANEOUS

Fluent in two languages	bilingual
Lasting only for a day	ephemeral
Word for word	verbatim
To change to stone	petrify
To reduce to powder	pulverise
A plane figure with six sides and six angles	hexagon
A plane figure with eight sides and eight angles	octagon
A plane figure with ten sides and ten angles	decagon
Sparing in eating and drinking	abstemious
Wasteful in spending	extravagant
To learn by heart	memorise
(Travelling) under a name other than one's own	incognito
Capable of being drawn out	malleable, ductile
Consisting of several kinds	miscellaneous
The exclusive right to buy or sell a commodity	monopoly
Unable to pay one's debts	insolvent
The outfit of a new-born baby	layette
Easily broken	fragile
Capable of being reduced to powder	friable

Miscellaneous (*contd.*)

Capable of being separated or torn asunder	discerptible
Close at hand	imminent
Serving for money	mercenary
Irresistible craving for alcoholic drinks	dipsomania
Excessive devotion to the female sex	gyneolatry
A fence or railing of stakes, or iron, etc.	palisade
A job for which one is paid, but which has few or no duties attached to it	sinecure
An appendix to a will	codicil
Correct spelling	orthography
Bad spelling	cacography
A line of people waiting for something	queue
Steps to enable one to get over a fence	stile
Loss of memory	amnesia
Loss of voice	aphonia, aphony
A seat on the back of an elephant	howdah
To turn a train etc. on a side track	shunting
The liquid which comes out from a sewerage tank	effluent
To separate the husks from the grain	winnow
A bar or pair of bars for confining cattle in a stall	stanchion
The likeness or representation of a person, especially on coins or medals	effigy
A foresaken or neglected child who has no home and spends most of its time on the streets	waif
The part of a receipt book, cheque book or money order retained by the issuer as a record	counterfoil, stub
An iron ring placed at the end of a staff to prevent it from splitting	ferrule
Living on flesh	carnivorous
Living on grass	herbivorous, graminivorous
Living on fish	piscivorous
Feeding on both animal and vegetable food, i.e. eating all kinds of food	omnivorous
A chairman's hammer	gavel

Miscellaneous (*contd.*)

A stick used by a music conductor, or by a policeman	baton
The yellow part of an egg	yolk
The white of an egg	albumen
The stripes on the sleeves of policemen and non-commissioned officers in the services to denote their rank	chevron
A bridge carrying a road or railway across a river or valley	viaduct
A mixture of metals, especially when an inferior metal is mixed with one of richer value	alloy
A rich covering over a throne or bed or carried over some dignitary in a procession	canopy
To lay a ship on its sides in order to clean it	careen
A fleet of merchant ships	argosy
Home-sickness or a sentimental longing for the past	nostalgia
A list of the various items of food to be served at a meal	menu
Directions for preparing certain dishes, sweetmeats, pastries etc.	recipe
The part of milk from which cheese is made	casein
Able to adapt oneself readily to many situations	versatile
Goods thrown overboard in order to make a ship lighter	jetsam
Goods found floating after a shipwreck	flotsam
A rally of Boy Scouts or a joyful gathering of youth groups	jamboree
A set of bells so arranged that tunes of songs or hymns can be played on them	carillon
A picture of a person or thing drawn in such a highly exaggerated manner as to cause laughter	caricature
An event occuring on the same date every year	anniversary
A line of persons or vehicles in order of arrival	queue
A beauty treatment used to darken the eyelashes and eyebrows	mascara
To pay off a debt by instalments	amortize
Able to use both hands with equal facility	ambidextrous
A name taken on by a person but which is not his real name	alias
A picture or pattern produced by putting together small pieces of coloured glass, marble or stone	mosaic

Miscellaneous (*contd.*)

A leather for sharpening razors	strop
A leather travelling-bag carried in the hand	valise
A list showing the order in which a number of persons have to perform certain duties	roster
One of a pair of baskets slung over the back of a donkey	pannier
A thing worn by some persons as a charm against evil, witchcraft, sickness etc.	amulet
The bony framework of the body	skeleton
The framework of a car	chassis
A covering of canvas, tarpaulin or other material to shade windows and doors from the sun	awning
To put to one's own use the money of another with which one is entrusted	embezzle
To be over-particular about spending of money	parsimonious
The space which for safety is left unfilled in a cask or vessel before it is sealed	ullage
A hollow space in a wall for a statue	niche
To compensate for loss or damage	indemnify
To bring a person before a court of law to answer a charge	arraign
An enclosure for prisoners in a courthouse	dock
The whole rim (or one of the segments of the rim) of a wheel	felloe
To divide into two equal parts	bisect
An income paid yearly	annuity
A boxer of the lightest class weighing 112 lbs or less	flyweight
A boxer who weighs between 113 and 118 lbs	bantamweight
A boxer who weighs between 118 and 121 lbs	featherweight
A boxer who weighs between 127 and 135 lbs	lightweight
A boxer who weighs between 136 and 147 lbs	welterweight
A boxer who weighs between 147 and 160 lbs	middleweight
A boxer who weighs between 160 and 175 lbs	light-heavyweight
A boxer who weighs over 175 lbs	heavyweight

FIGURATIVE EXPRESSIONS AND THEIR EXPLANATIONS

Above:
: *Above all*—chiefly, before everything else.
Above-board—not open to question, honest, straight-forward, beyond reproach.
Above-par—of superior quality.

Account:
: *On account of*—for the sake of.
On no account—not for any reason.
To give a good account of oneself—to act with credit to oneself.

Achates:
: *A fidus Achates*—a faithful friend.

Achilles:
: *The heel of Achilles*—a weak spot.
(Achilles, the famous Greek hero of the Iliad, when a child, had been dipped by his mother, Thetis, in the river Styx in order to make him invulnerable. The heel by which she held him was not touched by the water, and throughout his life this part of his body was his weak point. He was killed by Paris, who pierced his heel with an arrow.)

Adonis:
: *An Adonis*—a very handsome man.

Air:
: *To build castles in the air*—to think of something impossible of realisation; to day-dream; to conceive fanciful ideas.
To assume airs—to affect superiority.
To air one's opinions—to give vent to one's feelings in public.

Aloof:
: *To stand aloof*—to keep to oneself and not mix with others.

Altar:
: *To lead to the altar*—to marry.

Amazon:
: *An Amazon*—a warlike woman; a masculine woman.

Ananias:
: *An Ananias*—a liar (See Acts V 1–2).

Anchor: *To weigh anchor*——to be about to sail.
To cast anchor—to drop anchor into the sea; to fix oneself.

Apollo: *An Apollo*—a man with a perfect physique.

Apple: *The apple of discord*—a cause of strife, contention, or quarrel. (Eris the Goddess of Discord had not been invited to the wedding of Peleus and Thetis, the parents of Achilles. To avenge this slight, Eris threw among the guests a golden apple on which was written "For the most beautiful." Juno, Minerva and Venus contended for this prize of beauty and this quarrel finally led to the Trojan War.)
To upset the apple cart—to disturb the peace.
Apple pie order—in perfect order.

Apron: *To be tied to his mother's apron strings*—to be under the control and influence of his mother.

Arcadia: *Arcadian life*—a blissfully happy, rural and simple life. (Arcadia was a beautiful rural district in Greece, whose inhabitants led simple, happy lives.)

Arms: *To keep a person at arm's length*—to avoid coming in contact with a person, refuse to be on familiar terms with that person.
To take up arms—to fight; to go to war.
To receive with open arms—to welcome cordially.

Attic: *Attic salt*—refined, subtle wit, (for which the Athenians were famous).

Augean: *To cleanse the Augean stables*—to effect great improvements in government, or to abolish great abuses, in a very short time. (One of the twelve labours of Hercules was to clean the stables of Augeas, King of Elis, in which were 3,000 oxen and which stables had not been cleaned for thirty years. Hercules performed the task in a single day by leading the rivers Alpheus and Peneus through the farmyard.)

Axe: *To have an axe to grind*—to have some selfish objective in view.

B: *Not to know a B from a bull's foot*—to be ignorant of even the simplest things.

Babel: *A Babel*—a confused noise (see Genesis XI).

Back: *To break the back of anything*—to perform the most difficult part of it.
To get one's back up—to rouse one's anger.
To backbite a person—to slander or to speak ill of someone.
He is the backbone of his team—he is the one on whom his team mainly relies for its successes.
He has no backbone—he has no will of his own.
Backstairs influence—influence exerted in an underhand or clandestine manner.

Bad: *To cause bad blood*—to cause strife and enmity.
A bad egg; a bad penny—a worthless person.
Bad form—bad manners.

Bag: *Bag and baggage*—with all one's belongings.

Ball: *To keep the ball rolling*—to keep things going (esp. amusement); to keep up a conversation and prevent it from flagging.

Bandy: *To bandy words*—to wrangle or exchange arguments.

Baptism: *Baptism of fire*—a soldier's first experience of actual war.

Bar: *To call to the bar*—to admit as a barrister.

Barmecide: *Barmicide's feast*—imaginary benefits.

Bat: *Off one's own bat*—on one's own initiative.

Bear: *To bear down on*—to sail in the direction of.
To lose one's bearings—to be uncertain of one's position.

Beat: *To beat about the bush*—to approach a matter in an indirect and roundabout manner.
To be dead beat—worn out by fatigue.

Bed: *Bed and board*—lodgings and food.
As you make your bed, so you must lie on it—you will have to bear the consequences of your own mistakes or misdeeds.
To take to one's bed—to have to be confined to bed as a result of sickness.

Bee:	*To have a bee in one's bonnet*—to hold fantastic notions on some points; to be cranky. *Bee-line*—the shortest distance between two places.
Beg:	*To go a-begging*—to be sold very cheaply because no-one cares to buy.
Behind:	*Behind's one's back*—without one's knowledge. *Behind the scenes*—in private; out of sight.
Believe:	*To make believe*—to feign or pretend.
Bell:	*To bell the cat*—to do something which is extremely dangerous. To undertake a hazardous task with the object of rendering a common enemy harmless (from the fable of the Mice and the Cat).
Belt:	*To hit below the belt*—to act unfairly in a contest.
Berth:	*To give a person a wide berth*—to keep as far away from him as possible.
Better:	*His better half*—a man's wife.
Bird:	*A bird in the hand is worth two in the bush*—Certainty is better than possibility; the little that one actually possesses is of greater value than what one is only likely to obtain. *An old bird is not to be caught with chaff*—Experienced people are not easily fooled or deceived.
Bit:	*To take the bit between one's teeth*—to get out of control; to become unmanageable.
Bite:	*To bite the dust*—to be defeated in battle—to die. *The biter bit*—to cheat the cheater. *His bark was was worse that his bite*—He usually makes a lot of vain verbal threats.
Black:	*Let me see it in black and white*—Write it down.
Blanket:	*A wet blanket*—a person who discourages others; one who is a damper to enjoyment.
Blarney:	*To have kissed the blarney stone*—to have a very persuasive tongue.

Blood: *In cold blood*—deliberately; not in passion.
            Blood is thicker than water— One usually takes the side of one's relation against another who is not of one's own blood.

Blow: *To blow hot and cold*—to do one thing at one time and the opposite soon after.

Blue: *A blue stocking*—a learned woman, inclined to pedantry.
            Once in a blue moon—a very rare occurrence.
            Blue Ribbon—the highest prize in any sport competition or tournament.

Blush: *At first blush*—at first sight.

Boat: *In the same boat*—in the same misfortune or circumstances.

Bolt: *A bolt from the blue*—a sudden and unexpected occurrence.

Bone: *A bone of contention*—a cause of dispute.
            To have a bone to pick with someone—to have something to say to someone which might cause a quarrel.

Book: *A bookworm*—a person always poring over books.

Bound: *By leaps and bounds*—with remarkable speed.
            Homeward bound—on the way home.

Bowdlerise: *To Bowdlerise*—to remove all the objectionable passages from a book. (Thomas Bowdler in 1818 published an expurgated version of Shakespeare's works—hence the name.)

Boycott: *To boycott*—to avoid; to shun; to have no dealings with. (From Captain Boycott, an Irish Landlord, who was ostracised by members of the Irish Land League, owing to certain unpopular evictions which were carried out at his order.)

Breach: *Breach of promise*—failure to keep a promise to marry one to whom you are betrothed.

Bread:	*One's bread and butter*—one's means of livelihood.
	His bread is well buttered—He is in fortunate circumstances.
	The bread winner—one who provides the means of livelihood for himself and his family.
Break:	*To break in*—to tame; to bring under control in a gentle manner.
	To break the news—to reveal something unpleasant in a gentle manner.
	To break the ice—to be the first to begin; to take the first step.
Breast:	*To make a clean breast of anything*—to make a full confession.
Breathe:	*To breathe one's last*—to die.
	To breathe freely again—to be no longer in fear or anxiety.
Bricks:	*To make bricks without straw*—to attempt to do something without proper materials or due preparation.
Bridge:	*Never cross the bridge until you come to it*—Do not anticipate difficulties.
Bring:	*To bring down the house*—to cause rapturous applause.
	To bring up the rear—to be the last in line.
Broad:	*It is as broad as it is long*—It is the same whichever way you view it.
Brow:	*To knit the brow*—to frown.
	To brow beat—to bully.
Bucket:	*To kick the bucket*—to die.
Buckle:	*To buckle on one's armour*—to set to work energetically.
Bull:	*To take the bull by the horns*—to tackle any difficulty in a bold and direct manner.
John Bull:	*John Bull*—an Englishman.

Burke:	*To burke a question*—to suppress or prevent any discussion on it. (From a notorious Irish criminal named Burke who used to waylay people, suffocate them, and sell the bodies to the medical schools.)
Bury:	*To bury the hatchet*—to forget past quarrels and be friends again. (The American Indians had the custom of burying their tomahawks when peace was concluded, as a symbol of their peaceful intentions.)
Bush:	*Good wine needs no bush*—there is no need to advertise something good.
Busman:	*Busman's holiday*—one who elects to spend his holiday in an occupation similar to his regular work.
But:	*But me no buts*—Do not bring forward objections.
Cain:	*To raise Cain*—to rebuke severely.
Cake:	*To take the cake*—to take the first prize; to be the best of the lot.
Candle:	*To burn the candle at both ends*—to expend energy in two directions at the same time. *The game is not worth the candle*—The undertaking is not worth the trouble.
Canoe:	*To paddle your own canoe*—to be responsible for your actions; to act independently.
Cap:	*If the cap fits, wear it*—If you think the remarks made refer to you, then act accordingly. *To go cap in hand*—to beseech in a humble manner.
Capital:	*Capital punishment*—the death sentence or penalty. *Capital ship*—a warship of the most powerful kind.
Cart:	*To put the cart before the horse*—to do first what ought to be done afterwards; to reverse the proper order of things.
Cat:	*To let the cat out of the bag*—to expose the trick; to let out the secret.

To fight like cats and dogs—to be always quarrelling and fighting.

Care killed the cat—Don't worry and fret yourself to death.

See which way the cat jumps—Sit on the fence; see how things are likely to turn out before deciding on a course of action.

To rain cats and dogs—to rain incessantly.

He is a cat's paw—one used as a tool to do something dangerous. (In the fable the Monkey used the Cat's paw to pull chestnuts out of the fire.)

Catch: *To catch one's eye*—to attract attention.

Cerberus: *To give a sop to Cerberus*—to appease someone by gift or bribe; to bribe. (Cerberus was a three-headed dog supposed to guard the entrance to Hades and prevent the dead from escaping. When a person died, the Romans used to put a cake in his hand as a sop to Cerberus.)

Chair: *To take the chair*—to preside at a meeting.

Change: *To ring the changes*—to be continually making alterations and trying new methods.

Chauvinism: *Chauvinism*—absurd patriotism which manifests itself in warlike conduct. (From Nicholas Chauvin, a soldier ardently devoted to Napoleon.)

Chicken: *She is no chicken*—She is older than she says, or appears to be.

Chicken-hearted—weak, timid, cowardly.

Don't count your chickens before they are hatched—Don't calculate your gains before they are realised.

Chip: *A chip of the old block*—a son resembling his father in face, disposition, habits etc.

A chip on the shoulder—easily offended because of supposed grievance.

Chock: *Chock full*—full to overflowing.

Choice: *Hobson's choice*—no alternative; take what you are offered or none at all. (Hobson, a Cambridge livery-stable keeper, used to hire out horses, but insisted that the customer should take the first horse nearest the stable door, or none at all.)

Choose: *To pick and choose*—to make a careful selection.

Cicerone: *A Cicerone*—a guide who takes strangers and tourists over a country and explains to them all the curiosities and features of the place. (Cicero, the Roman orator, had an easy, flowing style.)

Cimmerian: *Cimmerian darkness*—profound darkness.

Circle: *To square the circle*—to attempt something impossible.

Close: *Close fisted*—mean, miserly.

Cloud: *Every cloud has a silver lining*—Adverse conditions do not last for ever; brighter days are usually in store.

To have one's head in the clouds—to live in dreamland; to have fanciful ideas.

Clover: *To live in clover; to be in clover*—to be living in great luxury.

Coals: *To carry coals to Newcastle*—to do anything superfluous or unnecessary. (Newcastle, a great coal port in England.)
To haul over the coals—to scold severely; to reprimand.
To heap coals of fire—to return good for evil (Prov. XXV 21-23).

Coast: *The coast is clear*—The danger is past: there is no danger of interference.

Coat: *Cut your coat according to your cloth*—Live within your income; make what you possess serve your needs.

Cock: *A cock and bull story*—a foolishly incredible story.
To be cock-sure—to be absolutely certain; extremely self-reliant.

Cold: *To throw cold water upon anything*—to discourage effort.

To give the cold shoulder—to rebuff, to treat with indifference.

Colour: *Off colour*—not in the usual form.
To show one's colours—to reveal one's true intentions by no longer pretending.
To come off with flying colours—to succeed brilliantly.

Commit: *To commit to memory*—to learn by heart.

Cook: *Too many cooks spoil the broth*—When there are more workers than necessary they are likely to get in each other's way and the result is apt to be a failure.

Coventry: *To send to Coventry*—to boycott; to refuse to be on familiar terms or to have any dealings with someone.

Crichton: *An admirable Crichton*—a very talented person.

Crocodile: *Crocodile tears*—hypocritical tears.

Crook: *By hook or crook*—by fair means or foul.

Crow: *As the crow flies*—in a direct line, the shortest distance between two points.

Cudgel: *To take up the cudgels*—to champion or fight for someone.

Curry: *To curry favour*—to seek favour by flattery.

Cut: *Cut and dry*—ready made.
To cut a dash—to make an impression.
A cut-throat—a murderer.

Dagger: *To be at daggers drawn*—to be deadly enemies.

Damocles: *To have the sword of Damocles hanging over one's head*—to be in imminent danger of losing one's life; to live in constant fear of some impending danger.

Daniel: *A Daniel*—an imperial judge. (Shakespeare, "Merchant of Venice"; Daniel I-VI.)

Dare: *A dare-devil*—a fearless, reckless man.

Date: *Up to date*—recent, modern.
Out of date—obsolete.

Davy: *In Davy Jones's locker*—drowned, at the bottom of the sea.

Day: *He has seen better days*—He was once prosperous.
          Evil days—a period of misfortune.
          To gain or win the day—to be victorious.
          Halcyon days—a time when there is peace and happiness in the land.

Dead: *Dead beat*—quite exhausted.
          Dead broke—penniless.
          To run dead heat—a race in which the contestants came in together.
          A dead letter—something which no longer exists.
          To step into dead men's shoes—to come into an inheritance; to succeed someone who died.

Devil: *To give the devil his due*—give a person credit for his good qualities however worthless he may be.
          Go to the devil—Be off.
          Devil's playthings—playing cards.
          Devil's bones—dice.
          To be between the devil and the deep sea—to be faced with two dangerous situations, each of which is to be dreaded as much as the other.
          Devil's advocate—one appointed by the Pope to oppose claims for canonisation; one who argues for the sake of argument by taking the opposite side.

Dilemma: *To be on the horns of a dilemma*—to be in such a position that it is difficult to decide what to do.

Dog: *Give a dog a bad name and hang him*—Once a person loses his reputation, he is likely to be blamed for the misdeeds of others.
          To be a dog in the manger—to prevent others from using what one cannot use oneself; to be selfish.
          Every dog has his day—Sooner or later, everyone has his share of good fortune.

Doldrums: *To be in the doldrums*—to be in low spirits; to be out of sorts.

Dole: *The Dole*—money given in charity, and also allowances to the unemployed.
To dole out—to give out in small quantities.

Door: *To keep the wolf from the door*—to avoid starvation.
To darken one's door—to pay a visit to one's house.

Down: *Ups and downs*—varying fortunes; changes and chances of life.
Down and out—penniless, ruined.

Draconian: *Draconian legislation*—very severe laws. (From Draco, an Athenian legislator, whose laws were extremely severe.)

Draw: *To draw the long bow*—to relate fantastic stories.
To draw the line at—to refuse to go beyond a certain limit.

Dust: *To throw dust in one's eyes*—to try to deceive someone.

Dutch: *Dutch courage*—bravery induced by alcoholic liquors.

Eagle: *Eagle-eye*—quick to discover; very discerning.

Ear: *To set by the ears*—to cause strife or incite to quarrel.

Eat: *To eat one's words*—to apologise; to take back what one has said.

Egg: *A bad egg*—a worthless person.
To egg on—to spur on to further action.
Do not put all your eggs in one basket—Do not stake all your money on a single industry. Spread your resources over a variety of transactions.

Elephant: *A white elephant*—a useless possession which is extremely expensive to keep (The Kings of Siam when they wished to ruin one of their courtiers presented him with a white elephant, an animal sacred in Siam. The cost of its upkeep was so ruinous that the wealth of the noble soon dwindled away.)

Eleven: *At the eleventh hour*—at the last moment.

Ell: *Give him an inch he'll take an ell*—He will abuse his privilege and take great liberties.

Elysian: *Elysian happiness*—a state of perfect bliss. (From Greek Mythology, Elysium, a region of perfect happiness whither the soul of the virtuous departed.)

End: *At his wit's end*—utterly confounded.
At the end of his tether—unable to proceed any farther.
Odds and ends—remnants.
To make both ends meet—to keep expenses within one's income.
Without end—everlasting.

Escutcheon: *A blot on the escutcheon*—a disgrace on the reputation of a family.

Exodus: *An exodus*—the departure of a large body of people. (From the Exodus of the Israelites from Egypt under Moses.)

Eye: *An eye for an eye*—tit for tat; to return evil for evil; retaliate.
To keep an eye on—to watch carefully.
To see eye to eye—to be in complete agreement with the views of another.

Fabian: *Fabian tactics*—a policy of wearing down an opponent by delaying action; harassing an enemy by avoiding open battle. (Fabius Maximus, a Roman Consul, wore down Hannibal by refraining from engaging him in actual battle in the second Punic War.)

Face: *To save one's face*—to avoid disgrace.

Fair: *The fairer sex*—women.

Faith: *Bad faith*—dishonest intentions.
In good faith—with honest intentions.
A breach of faith—to act contrary to what one had professed.

Fall: *To fall out*—to quarrel.
To fall through—to fail.
To fall upon—to attack.

False: *To sail under false colours*—to attempt to deceive.

Feather: *A feather in one's cap*—an honour; a distinction.
Birds of a feather flock together—People of similar tastes and dispositions crave each other's company.
To feather one's nest—to provide for the future.
To show the white feather—to show signs of cowardice.

Fence: *To sit on the fence*—to remain neutral; to take neither side in a controversy.

Fiddle: *As fit as a fiddle*—in excellent health.
To play second fiddle—to take a subordinate position.

File: *To march in single, or Indian file*—to march in a single line, one behind another.

Finger: *To have at one's finger-tips*—to know thoroughly.

Fire: *To set the Thames on fire*—to do something sensational or remarkable.
Fire away—Begin; say what you want to say.
To spread like wild fire—to circulate (of news) with astonishing speed.
A burnt child dreads the fire—One who has had a previous unpleasant experience is always scared of situations where such experiences are likely to be repeated.

Fish: *A fish out of water*—anyone in an awkward embarrassing situation.
Other fish to fry—more important business to attend to.
This story is fishy—The truth of the story is doubtful.
All is fish that comes to his net—He is not over particular about propriety.

Fit: *By fits and starts*—spasmodically; not continuous; intermittently.

Flare: *To flare up*—to fly into a passion.

Flash: *A flash in the pan*—a sudden, single success.

Flog: *To flog a dead horse*—to try to revive interest in something already stale and beyond hope of resuscitation.

Foot: *To carry one off his feet*—to cause one to be intoxicated with admiration.
To foot the bill—to pay the bill.
To put one's foot in it—to get into trouble.
To put one's foot down—to put a stop to.

Foregone: *A foregone conclusion*—a decision arrived at beforehand.

Fortune: *Hostages to fortune*—one's wife and children.

Foul: *Foul play*—unfair dealing in a game: cheating.

French: *To take French leave*—to leave one's companions furtively and without notice.

Fry: *To jump from the frying-pan into the fire*—to come out of one trouble and get into a worse.

Gain: *To gain ground*—to make progress in any undertaking.
To gain the upper hand—to have the advantage.

Gallery: *To play to the gallery*—to endeavour to gain cheap popularity.

Game: *The game is up*—All is lost; everything has failed.
To have the game in one's hand—to be certain of winning.
To play the game—to act fairly and honourably.

Gargantua: *A gargantuan appetite*—an enormous appetite. (François Rabelais in his book "Gargantua and Pantagruel" narrates the adventures of two mythical giants. So great was Gargantua, that even when a baby a day old, 17 913 cows were required to furnish him with milk.)

Gauntlet: *To take up the gauntlet*—to accept the challenge.
To throw down the gauntlet—to challenge.
To run the gauntlet—to receive blows from all sides; to be criticised on all quarters.

Ghost: *To give up the ghost*—to die; to cease trying.

Gift: *Do not look a gift-horse in the mouth*—Do not examine a gift too critically; do not criticise what is given for nothing; accept a gift for the sentiments which inspire it, and not for its value.

Glass: *Those who live in glass houses should not throw stones*—People who do not live blameless lives should not find fault with others.

Gnat: *To strain at a gnat and swallow a camel*—to be over particular in small things and lax in more important issues.

Gold: *All that glisters is not gold*—Things are not always as attractive as they appear.

Good: *A good-for-nothing*—a worthless person.
            A good Samaritan—a friend in need. (St. Luke X 33.)

Goose: *A wild-goose chase*—a vain attempt.
            To kill the goose that laid the golden egg—to lose a valuable source of income through greed.

Gordian: *To cut the Gordian knot*—to solve a difficult problem by adopting bold or drastic measures.

Grade: *To grade up*—to improve the stock by crossing with a better breed.

Green: *He has a green eye*—He is jealous.
            To give the green light—to give approval to proceed.

Grist: *To bring grist to the mill*—to bring profitable business or gain.

Hairs: *To split hairs*—to argue about unimportant issues.

Hand: *From hand to hand*—from one person to another.
            To take a person in hand—to undertake to correct a person of his faults; to discipline.
            To live from hand to mouth—to spend all one's earnings; to make no provision for the future.

Hard: *Hard and fast rules*—strict rules.
            Hard of hearing—almost deaf.
            A die-hard—one who yields a point only after a struggle.

Hare: *To run with the hare and hunt with the hounds*—to act treacherously; to play both sides.

Harness: *Back in harness*—to resume work after a holiday.
To die in harness—to continue at one's occupation until death.

Harp: *To harp on the same string*—to refer repeatedly to the same subject.

Haste: *More haste less speed*—Work done hurriedly is apt to be badly done, necessitating the job being done all over again. The overall time spent is usually more than if the job had been carefully done from the start.

Hat: *To hang up one's hat*—to make oneself comfortable in another person's home.
To pass the hat around—to ask for subscriptions.

Hay: *Make hay while the sun shines*—Take advantage of all opportunities.

Head: *To keep one's head on*—to remain calm.
To lose one's head—to be carried away by excitement.
Uneasy lies the head that wears a crown—rulers and other people in authority have no easy time—their responsibilities weigh heavily upon them.

Heart: *To have one's heart in one's mouth*—to be afraid.
His heart is in his boots—he is a coward.

Hector: *To hector a person*—to bully someone.

Heels: *To show a clean pair of heels*—to run at a great speed.
To take to one's heels—to run at great speed.

Hermetically sealed: *Hermetically sealed*—sealed closely and perfectly so as to exclude air.

Herod: *To out-Herod Herod*—to outdo someone in something for which he is noted.

High: *On one's high horse*—arrogant; affecting superiority.
With a high hand—in a dictatorial or arbitrary manner.
High-flown language—bombastic language.

Hole: *To pick holes in*—to find fault with.

Hoof: *To show the cloven hoof*—to reveal one's evil intentions.

Hook: *By hook or crook*—by fair means or foul.

Horse: *Straight from the horse's mouth*—from the most reliable source.

               To flog a dead horse—to attempt to put life into a movement which is past all hopes of resuscitation; to make fruitless efforts.

               Horse of a different colour—another matter altogether.

Hot: *To be in hot water*—to be in trouble or difficulty.

Hour: *At the eleventh hour*—at the last moment.
               The darkest hour is nearest the dawn—Relief is often just around the corner when things appear at their blackest.

Humble: *To eat humble pie*—to submit oneself to humiliation and insult; to apologise humbly; to take an inferior place.

Ice: *To break the ice*—to take the first step in an awkward situation; to lead the way when others are hesitant to come forward.

Ignorance: *Where ignorance is bliss 'tis folly to be wise*—It is foolish to try to educate people who are happy to remain in their state of ignorance.

Iron: *To have too many irons in the fire*—to be attempting too many projects at the same time.
               An iron-bound coast—a coast surrounded by rocks.
               Strike while the iron is hot—take advantage of favourable opportunities.

Jezebel: *A Jezebel*—a wicked, bold or vicious woman—especially one who paints her face. (From wife of Ahab, King of Israel.)

Jiffy: *In a jiffy*—in an exceedingly short time.

Jowl: *Cheek by jowl*—with cheeks close together; close together.

Kin: *Next of kin*—nearest of blood relation.

Kind: (*To give or pay*) *in kind*—to give or pay in produce or commodities, not in money.

Kiss: *To kiss the book*—to take an oath in a court of law by touching the Bible with the lips.
To kiss the dust—to be defeated in battle; to be slain.

Kowtow: *To kowtow to anyone*—to act in a very servile manner.

Laconic: *A laconic speech*—a concise, pithy, epigrammatic speech.

Laurels: *To look to one's laurels*—to take care not to lose one's place; to guard against defeat by a rival.
To win laurels—to gain distinction or glory in a contest.
To rest on one's laurels—to retire from active life after gaining distinction or glory in the field of sports, athletics etc.

Lamp: *To smell of the lamp*—to show signs of strenuous preparation for an examination or a speech etc.

Law: *To go to law*—to take legal proceedings.
To take the law into one's hands—to try to gain revenge or satisfaction by force, and without recourse to the law courts.

Leaf: *To take a leaf out of one's book*—to imitate, to follow the example of another.

To turn over a new leaf—to change one's mode of life or conduct for the better.

Leap: *Look before you leap*—think before acting.

Leg: *To be on one's last legs*—to be on the verge of ruin.
To stand on one's own legs—to depend entirely on one's own resources; to be independent.

Lie: *To give the lie to*—to prove to be false.
A white lie—an excusable untruth.
Let sleeping dogs lie—Do not recall matters which are likely to cause pain or grief or embarrassment to those concerned.

Light:
: *To bring to light*—to reveal, to disclose, to bring to public notice.
To come to light—to become known.
To see the light—to understand; to be converted.
To throw some light upon—to explain.
To make light of—to treat slightly; to disregard.

Lilliputian:
: *A Lilliputian*—a pygmy; a very short person.

Lines:
: *Hard lines*—a hard lot, to be in an extremely unenviable position.
To read between the lines—to detect the hidden meaning.

Lion:
: *The lion's share*—the largest part; almost the whole.
To beard the lion in his den—to defy a tyrant in his own domain; to resist openly one who is generally feared.
To twist the lion's tail—to insult or provoke someone of power.

Lock:
: *Lock, stock and barrel*—the whole of everything.

Loggerhead:
: *To be at loggerheads*—to be constantly arguing or quarrelling.

Long:
: *Before long*—soon; in a short while.
In the long run—eventually.
The long and short of it—everything summed up in a few words.

Look:
: *Look before you leap*—Think carefully before acting.
To look down upon—to spurn, despise, or think someone inferior.

Lurch:
: *To leave in the lurch*—to desert someone still in difficulties.

Machiavellian policy:
: A policy in which any means, however unscrupulous or treacherous, may be employed to achieve the end.

Malapropism:
: A grotesque misuse of words. (From Mrs. Malaprop in Sheridan's "The Rivals".)

Marines:
: *Tell it to the marines*—I don't believe your story.

Mark:	*Not up to the mark*—not measuring up to a required standard. *To make one's mark*—to distinguish oneself; succeed brilliantly. *To be beside the mark, to be wide of the mark*—to miss the point completely.
Martinet:	*A martinet*—a very strict disciplinarian. (From Jean Martinet, a very strict officer under Louis XIV.)
Means:	*By all means*—certainly. *By any means*—in any way possible. By no means—on no account whatever.
Medes:	*The laws of the Medes and Persians*—unalterable laws.
Mercury:	*A Mercurial temperament*—light-hearted; fickle; flighty.
Miss:	*A miss is as good as a mile*—The result is the same whether a person just misses the mark he has aimed at, or comes nowhere near it.
Morpheus:	*In the arms of Morpheus*—asleep.
Move:	*To move heaven and earth*—to exert all efforts; to leave no stone unturned.
Much:	*Much of a muchness*—almost alike; practically the same.
Nail:	*Nail the lie to the counter*—expose it publicly. *To hit the nail on the head*—to mention the true facts of a case; to come up with the right answers.
Needle:	*To look for a needle in a haystack*—to begin a search for something with only a slim chance of success.
Nick:	*In the nick of time*—at the right moment; just before too late.
Nine:	*A stitch in time saves nine*—If we give due attention to the little details of life, in the long run we will save ourselves from considerable time, worry and expense.

Nose:
: *To lead by the nose*—to lead blindly.
To turn up one's nose—to express contempt.
To put one's nose into something—to be unduly meddlesome.
Under one's nose—under one's close observation.

Nut:
: *A hard nut to crack*—a person difficult to convince; a problem difficult to solve.
In a nutshell—summed up in a few words.
To put in a nutshell—to express in very concise terms; to say in a few words.

Oil:
: *To pour oil on troubled waters*—to make peace.

Olive:
: *To hold out the olive branch*—to ask for peace.

Out:
: *Out of sorts*—unwell.
Out of temper—angry.
Out of the wood—out of danger.

P:
: *To mind one's P's and Q's*—to be very particular about one's behaviour. (In the old days in the ale house the host used to mark up the pints and quarts consumed by his customers on the wall or a blackboard. It therefore behoved the customer to mind his P(ints) and Q(uarts) in order that he did not get overcharged.)

Pass:
: *To come to pass*—to happen.
To pass on—to proceed.

Pave:
: *To pave the way*—to facilitate.

Pay:
: *To pay the piper*—to pay the expense.

Parthian:
: *Parthian shot*—a parting word; a sharp retort at the end of a conversation.

Pearls:
: *To cast pearls before swine*—to bestow good things upon people who cannot appreciate them.

Penny:
: *In for a penny, in for a pound*—since I am to attempt a little I might as well attempt a lot.

Peter:
: *To rob Peter to pay Paul*—to take what belongs to one person and pay another; to satisfy one person at the expense of another.

Petticoat: *Petticoat government*—to be under the rule of a female, especially a wife or mother.

Pick: *To pick to pieces*—to analyse critically.

Pig: *To buy a pig in a poke*—to purchase something on mere reputation and without examining it beforehand.

Pin: *To pin one's faith on*—to rely on.
              Pin money—originally a husband's allowance to his wife for dress, toilet necessaries, etc. Now a negligible amount.

Plough: *To put one's hand to the plough*—to begin a task earnestly.
              To plough the sands—to labour uselessly.
              To plough a lonely furrow—to hold a view opposed to all your associates; to pursue with determination an unusual course of action or branch of study.

Point: *To make a point of something*—to attach special importance to doing something.
              To the point—fit; appropriate; relevant.

Pooh: *To pooh-pooh an idea*—to express contempt for an idea.

Port: *Any port in a storm*—When one is in great difficulty one looks for help from any quarter.

Pot: *To take pot-luck*—to share in a meal not specially prepared for guests.

Pudding: *The proof of the pudding is in the eating*—People are judged by their actions.

Pull: *To pull down a person*—to degrade or humiliate a person.
              To pull to pieces—to criticise.
              To pull through—to pass an examination, or succeed in something after a great deal of difficulty.
              To pull together—to co-operate.
              To pull strings—to court the favour of highly placed officials in order to secure remunerative jobs or positions.

Pulse: *To feel one's pulse*—to try to find out one's views or intentions.

Purse: *An empty purse, a light purse*—poverty.
A heavy purse—wealth or riches.
To hold the purse strings—to have control of finance.
To make a silk purse out of a sow's ear—to attempt to accomplish great things with inferior materials.

Pyrrhic: *Pyrrhic victory*—a victory that is as costly as defeat.

Quandary: *To be in a quandary*—to be in an unenviable position.

Queer: *To be in Queer Street*—to be in an embarrassing position; to be in trouble.

Question: *Out of the question*—not worth discussing or considering.
To pop the question—to propose marriage.

Qui Vive: *To be on the qui vive*—to be on the look out; to be on the alert.

Quixotic: *To be quixotic*—to be extremely romantic, with very lofty but impractical ideals. (From Don Quixote, hero of the romance "Don Quixote" by Cervantes.)

Rain: *It never rains but it pours*—Good fortune is usually the forerunner of great prosperity; similarly a streak of bad luck is just the beginning of great misfortune.

Rat: *To be like a drowned rat*—to be soaking wet.
To smell a rat—to suspect something.

Reckoning: *Days of reckoning*—the time when one will have to settle accounts, or to give some account of one's work.

Record: *To break the record*—to surpass all previous achievements in competition, especially in the field of sports.

Red: *Red flag*—the symbol of revolution, a sign of danger.

To be caught red-handed—to be caught in the very act of committing a crime.

To draw a red-herring across the trail—to turn attention from the real issue by irrelevant discussion.

Red-letter day—a memorable day; a day of great importance.

Red-tape—a term used to describe the delay in attending to matters in government departments because of official routine and formality.

Rein:
To give rein to—to allow a person to have his own way.

To take the reins—to assume command.

Rome:
Rome was not built in a day—It takes time to accomplish anything really worthwhile. (Rome was the capital city of the great Roman Empire.)

Rope:
To give (a person) plenty of rope—to allow a person to act as he pleases in order that he may commit some blunder.

To know the ropes—to be thoroughly acquainted with the particular situation.

Rough:
To rough it—to put up with inconveniences and hardships.

Rough and ready—hastily prepared, without neatness or adornment.

Rough and tumble—in a disorderly manner.

To ride roughshod over—to treat in a high-handed fashion.

Rubber:
To win the rubber—to win the majority of a given set of matches in a tournament, e.g. cricket.

Rubicon:
To cross the Rubicon—to take a decisive step from which there is no turning back; to cast the die.

Salt:
Below the salt—in the company of the less distinguished.

To take with a grain of salt—to accept with doubt or misgiving.

Samaritan:
To be a good Samaritan—to be kind and compassionate to someone in distress.

Sauce: *What is sauce for the goose is sauce for the gander*—The conditions are the same for all parties concerned.

Score: *To pay off old scores*—to have one's revenge for an offence of long standing.

Scylla: *To be between Scylla and Charybdis*—to be faced with two dangerous alternatives, so that escape from one will involve ruin from the other.

See: *To see daylight*—to begin to understand.
To see red—to be mad with anger.

Shave: *A close shave*—a narrow escape.

Shoulder: *To give the cold shoulder*—to ignore or treat with contempt.

Silk: *To take silk*—to become a Q.C. (Queen's Counsel).

Skeleton: *A skeleton in the cupboard, the family skeleton*—a dreadful domestic secret.

Skin: *By the skin of the teeth*—very narrowly.
To save one's skin—to escape harm or injury.

Snake: *A snake in the grass*—an enemy who strikes under cover.

Spartan: *A Spartan life*—a life of extreme self-discipline, aimed at promoting health of body and mind.

Spade: *To call a spade a spade*—to be brutally frank, outspoken, blunt in speech.

Spick and span: *Spick and span*—smart and clean.

Sponge: *To throw in the sponge*—to acknowledge defeat.

Steal: *To steal a march on*—to go ahead of; to go beforehand.

Stone: *A rolling stone gathers no moss*—Unstable people never achieve anything worthwhile; people who cannot settle down to business are never successful.

Straw: *A man of straw*—one who has no financial resources.

Sunday: *A month of Sundays*—an indefinitely long period.

Swallow: *One swallow does not make a summer*—It is unreliable to base one's conclusions on only a single test or incident.

Tables: *To turn the tables*—to reverse the conditions.

Tail: *To turn tail*—to desert, to run away.

Tangent: *To go off at a tangent, to fly off at a tangent*—to change suddenly to a different course of thought or action.

Tapis: *On the tapis*—under consideration.

Tar: *To spoil the ship for a ha'p'orth of tar*—to ruin something extremely valuable by failure to spend trifling sums on maintenance and repairs.

Tenterhooks: *To be on tenterhooks*—to be in a state of suspense and anxiety.

Thespian: *Thespian art*—the art of tragedy or drama.

Towel: *To throw in the towel*—to acknowledge defeat.

Town: *Man about town*—a well-dressed idler who frequents nightclubs and places of entertainment.

Triton: *A triton among the minnows*—a person who completely dominates all his fellows.

Turtle: *To turn turtle*—to overturn, to make a complete somersault.

Vessels: *Empty vessels make the most noise*—Those who know or have little often shout the loudest.

Wheel: *To put one's shoulder to the wheel*—to work hard in order to succeed.

Wind: *To take the wind out of one's sails*—to frustrate by using a person's own materials or methods.

Wire: *Wire-pulling*—to exercise an influence felt but not seen.

Wishes: *If wishes were horses, beggars might ride*—If all people's wishes came true everybody would be rich.

Wonder: *A nine days' wonder*—an event which creates a sensation for a time but is soon forgotten.

Wool: *To pull the wool over one's eyes*—to mislead or deceive.

Yellow: *Yellow press*—newspapers which publish sensational and unscrupulous stories about crime, sex, etc.

PROVERBS

A bad beginning makes a good ending.
A bad excuse is better than none at all.
A bad husband cannot be a good man.
A beggar can never be bankrupt.
A bird in the hand is worth two in the bush.
A burnt child dreads fire.
A cat may look at a king.
A cheerful look makes a dish a feast.
A cheerful wife is the joy of life.
A clear conscience is a coat of mail.
A drowning man will catch at a straw.
A drunkard's purse is a bottle.
A fault confessed is half redressed.
A fool and his money are soon parted.
A fool may give a wise man counsel.
A fool may make money, but it takes a wise man to spend it.
A friend in need is a friend indeed.
A friend is easier lost than found.
A friend's frown is better than a fool's smile.
A full purse makes the mouth to speak.
A good dog deserves a good bone.
A good horse seldom needs the spur.
A good husband makes a good wife.
A good name is better than riches.
A good name is sooner lost than won.
A great talker is a great liar.
A guilty conscience needs no accuser.
A hungry man is an angry man.
A heavy purse makes a light heart.
A man in debt is caught in a net.
A man is as old as he feels.
A man's house is his castle.
A miss is as good as a mile.

A penny for your thoughts.
A penny saved is a penny gained.
A pound of care won't pay an ounce of debt.
A rolling stone gathers no moss.
A rose between two thorns.
A short cut is often a wrong cut.
A stitch in time saves nine.
A thing begun is half done.
A wise man changes his mind sometimes, a fool never.
A wonder lasts nine days.
A word to the wise is enough.
Absence makes the heart grow fonder.
Action speaks louder than words.
Advice when most needed is least heeded.
After a storm comes a calm.
All covet, all lose.
All that glisters is not gold.
All work and no play makes Jack a dull boy.
All play and no work makes Jack a mere toy.
All's fair in love and war.
All's fish that comes to his net.
All's well that ends well.
Among the blind the one-eyed man is king.
An apple a day keeps the doctor away.
An army marches on its stomach.
An empty bag will not stand upright.
An idle brain is the devil's workshop.
An old bird is not to be caught with chaff.
An ounce of discretion is worth a pound of wit.
An ounce of a prevention is worth a pound of cure.
Any port in a storm.
Appetite comes with eating.
As a man lives so shall he die.
As well be hanged for a sheep as a lamb.
As you make your bed so you must lie on it.
As you sow, so you shall reap.
Ask much to get little.
Avoid evil and it will avoid thee.
Back again, like a bad penny.

Barking dogs seldom bite.
Be just before you are generous.
Be not the first to quarrel, nor the last to make it up.
Be sure before you marry, of a house wherein to tarry.
Beggars must not be choosers.
Better be alone than in ill company.
Better late than never.
Better be happy than wise.
Between the devil and the deep blue sea.
Birds of a feather flock together.
Blood is thicker than water.
Books and friends should be few and good.
Borrowing thrives but once.
Boys will be boys.
Brevity is the soul of wit.
Bullies are generally cowards.
By others' faults wise men correct their own.
By timely mending save much spending.
Call a spade a spade.
Care killed the cat.
Catch not at the shadow and lose the substance.
Catch the bear before you sell his skin.
Catch who catch can.
Charity begins at home but should not end there.
Cheapest is dearest.
Children are what you make them.
Christmas comes but once a year.
Comparisons are odious.
Courtesy costs nothing.
Curses are like chickens, they come home to roost.
Cut your coat according to your cloth.
Dead men tell no tales.
Delays are dangerous.
Devil takes the hindmost.
Diligence is a great teacher.
Discretion is the better part of valour.
Distance lends enchantment to the view.
Do as I say, not as I do.
Do not cut off your nose to spite your face.

Do not put all your eggs in one basket.
Do not count your chickens before they are hatched.
Do not spur a willing horse.
Do not tell tales out of school.
Early to bed and early to rise,
     Makes a man healthy, wealthy and wise.
Easier said than done.
Eat to live, but do not live to eat.
Employment brings enjoyment.
Empty vessels make the most noise.
Enough is as good as a feast (to one that's not a beast).
Enough is better than too much.
Every ass loves to hear himself bray.
Every cloud has a silver lining.
Every dog has his day.
Every little helps.
Every man has his price.
Every man for himself and God for us all.
Every man must carry his own cross.
Every man has his weakness.
Every why has a wherefore.
Everyone can find fault, few can do better.
Everyone knows best where the shoe pinches.
Everyone thinks his own burden the heaviest.
Everyone thinks he is best able to advise others.
Everything comes to those who wait.
Example is better than precept.
Exchange is no robbery.
Experience teaches.
Experience keeps a dear school, but fools will learn in no other.
Extremes are dangerous.
Facts are stubborn things.
Failure teaches success.
Faint heart never won a fair lady.
Fall out with a friend for a trifle.
Familiarity breeds contempt.
Fancy kills and fancy cures.
Fine feathers make fine birds.
Fingers were made before forks.
Fire is a good servant but a bad master.

First come first served.

Flattery brings friends, truth enemies.

Flies are easier caught with honey than with vinegar.

Follow the river and you will find the sea.

Fools build houses and wise men buy them.

Forewarned is forearmed.

Fortune favours the brave.

Fortune favours fools.

Genius is a capacity for taking trouble.

Give a dog a bad name and hang him.

Give a fool rope enough and he will hang himself.

Give and spend and God will send.

Give everyone his due.

Give him an inch and he'll take an ell.

Give the devil his due.

God helps those who help themselves.

God never shuts one door but he opens another.

Good beginnings make good endings.

Good to begin well, better to end well.

Good wine needs no bush.

Grasp all, lose all.

Gratitude is the least of virtues, ingratitude the worst of vices.

Great haste makes great waste.

Great minds think alike.

Great profits, great risks.

Great talkers are little doers.

Habit is second nature.

Hail fellow, well met.

Half a loaf is better than no bread.

Hasty climbers have sudden falls.

He giveth twice that gives in a trice.

He is idle that might be better employed.

He is richest that has fewest wants.

He knows most who speaks least.

He knows which way the wind blows.

He laughs best that laughs last.

He runs with the hounds and hunts with the hare.

He that by the plough would thrive,
    Himself must either hold or drive.

He that comes first to the hill, may sit where he will.

He that doth lend doth lose his friend.

He that goes-a-borrowing, goes a-sorrowing.

He that knows little soon repents it.

He that knows nothing, doubts nothing.

He that loves glass without G,
>   Takes away L, and that is he.

He that will eat the kernel must crack the nut.

He that will not when he may,
>   When he will he shall have nay.

He that will thrive must rise at five,
>   He that hath thriven may lie till seven.

He who ceases to pray ceases to prosper.

He who likes borrowing dislikes paying.

He's no man who cannot say "No".

His bark is worse than his bite.

His heart is in his boots.

Home is home, though it never be so homely.

Honest men marry soon, wise men not at all.

Honesty is the best policy.

Hope is the last thing that we lose.

Hope springs eternal in the human breast.

Hunger is the best sauce.

If a man deceive me once, shame on him; if twice, shame on me.

If fools went not to market bad wares would not be sold.

If the cap fits, wear it.

If the mountain will not go to Mahomet, Mahomet must go to the
>   mountain.

If wishes were horses, beggars might ride.

If you cannot make a man think as you do, make him do as you think.

If you wish for peace, prepare for war.

Ill got, ill spent.

In for a penny, in for a pound.

It is a good horse that never stumbles, and a good wife that never
>   grumbles.

It is a long lane that has no turning.

It is always time to do good.

It is an ill wind that blows nobody good.

It is easier to get money than to keep it.

It is easier to pull down than to build.

It is easy to be wise after the event.

It is folly to live in Rome, and strive with the Pope.
It is never too late to mend.
It is no use crying over spilt milk.
It never rains but it pours.
It takes two to make a quarrel.
Jack of all trades and master of none.
Kill not the goose that lays the golden eggs.
Kill two birds with one stone.
Kind words are worth much and cost little.
Kindle not a fire that you cannot put out.
Kindness begets kindness.
Kissing goes by favour.
Knowledge is power.
Lazy people take the most pains.
Learning makes the wise wiser, but the fool more foolish.
Least said, soonest mended.
Lend only what you can afford to lose.
Let bygones be bygones.
Let sleeping dogs lie.
Let the cobbler stick to his last.
Liars should have good memories.
Life is never one sweet song.
Like father, like son. Like mother, like daughter.
Little boats must keep the shore,
    Larger boats may venture more.
Little strokes fell great oaks.
Live and let live.
Live not to eat, but eat to live.
Loans and debts make worries and frets.
Look before you leap.
Lost time is never found.
Love is blind.
Make every bargain clear and plain,
    That none may afterwards complain.
Make hay while the sun shines.
Make short the miles, with talk and smiles.
Man proposes, God disposes.
Manners maketh man.
Many find fault without an end,
    And yet do nothing at all to mend.

Many hands make light work.

Many straws may bind an elephant.

Marry in haste, repent at leisure.

Masters two, will not do.

Men are as old as they feel; women as old as they look.

Men make houses, women make homes.

Misfortunes never (seldom) come singly.

Money makes the mare to go.

More haste, less speed.

Much cry, little wool. (Great cry, little wool.)

Murder will out.

Nature abhors a vacuum.

Nearest is dearest.

Necessity hath no law.

Necessity is the mother of invention.

Needles and pins, needles and pins,
    When a man's married then trouble begins.

Neither wise men nor fools can work without tools.

Never a rose without thorns.

Never cross the bridge until you have come to it.

Never damn the bridge that you have crossed.

Never do things by halves.

Never hit a man when he's down.

Never look a gift horse in the mouth.

Never put off till tomorrow what may be done today.

Never say die! Up man, and try.

Never spoil the ship for a ha'p'orth of tar.

Never too old to learn; never too late to turn.

Never trouble trouble till trouble troubles you.

New brooms sweep clean.

No gains without pains.

No living man, all things can.

No man is indispensable.

No man is without enemies.

No news is good news.

No-one knows where the shoe pinches but he who wears it.

None so blind as those who will not see.

None so deaf as those who will not hear.

Nothing succeeds like success.

Nothing venture, nothing have—win.

Oaks fall when reeds stand.
Of one ill come many.
Of two evils choose the less.
Old age is a heavy burden.
Old birds are not caught with chaff.
Old wounds soon bleed.
On a long journey even a straw is heavy.
One can live on a little, but not on nothing.
One cannot die twice.
One fool makes many.
One good turn deserves another.
One may lead a horse to water, but twenty cannot make him drink.
One man's meat is another man's poison.
One may sooner fall than rise.
One swallow does not make a summer.
One today is worth two tomorrows.
Other fish to fry.
Out of debt, out of danger.
Out of sight, out of mind.
Out of the frying pan into the fire.
Penny wise, pound foolish.
Pigs grow fat where lambs would starve.
Plaster thick, some will stick.
Practice makes perfect.
Practise thrift or else you'll drift.
Praise makes good men better and bad men worse.
Presents keep friendships warm.
Prevention is better than cure.
Pride and poverty are ill, yet often dwell together.
Pride must (or will) have a fall.
Pride goes before a fall.
Procrastination is a thief of time.
Punctuality is the soul of business.
Punctuality is the politeness of princes.
Put not your trust in money; put your money in trust.
Put your own shoulder to the wheel.
Quick believers need broad shoulders.
Rats desert a sinking ship.
Reckless youth makes rueful age.
Rome was not built in a day.

Rumour is a great traveller.
Save me from my friends.
Saying is one thing, doing another.
Scratch my back and I will scratch yours.
Second thoughts are best.
See a pin and let it lie,
    You're sure to want before you die.
Seeing is believing.
Set a thief to catch a thief.
Set not your loaf in till the oven is hot.
She's the cat's mother.
Show me a liar and I'll show you a thief.
Silence gives consent.
Sink or swim.
Six of one and half a dozen of the other.
Skill is stronger than strength.
Sloth makes all things difficult, but industry all easy.
Slow and steady wins the race.
Slow and sure.
Small beginnings make great endings.
Soft words break no bones.
Soft words win hard hearts.
Some men are wise and some are otherwise.
Sometimes the best gain is to lose.
Soon hot, soon cold.
Sooner said than done.
Spare the rod and spoil the child.
Speak little but speak the truth.
Speak well of your friends, and of your enemy nothing.
Speaking without thinking is shooting without aim.
Speech is silver, silence is golden.
Spilt salt is never all gathered.
Still water runs deep.
Strike while the iron's hot.
Study the past if you would divine the future.
Suspicion is the bane of friendship.
Sympathy without relief is like mustard without beef.
Take care of the pence and the pounds will take care of themselves.
Talk of the devil and he'll appear.

That which is evil is soon learnt.
That which proves too much proves nothing.
The best of friends must part.
The biter bit.
The cat is fain the fish to eat, but hath no will to wet her feet.
The cheapest comes the dearest in the end.
The child is father of the man.
The company makes the feast.
The darkest hour is nearest the dawn.
The devil lurks behind the cross.
The early bird catches the worm.
The end justifies the means.
The exception proves the rule.
The fountain is clearest at its source.
The game is not worth the candle.
The goat must browse where she is tied.
The habit does not make the monk.
The heart sees further than the head.
The last straw breaks the camel's back.
The less people think, the more they talk.
The love of a woman and a bottle of wine
    Are sweet for a season but last for a time.
The master's eye fattens the horse.
The morning sun never lasts the day.
The nearer the church the further from God.
The proof of the pudding is in the eating.
The public pays with ingratitude.
The receiver is as bad as the thief.
The stone that lieth not in your way need not offend you.
The strength of a chain is its weakest link.
The tongue ever turns to the aching tooth.
The unexpected always happens.
The wise make jests and the fool repeats them.
The wish is father to the thought.
The world is a staircase; some are going up, some are coming down.
There are as good fish in the sea as ever came out of it.
There are more foolish buyers than foolish sellers
There are more ways to kill a dog than by hanging him.
There are two sides to every question.
There could be no great ones if there were no little.

There is a "But" in everything.
There is no true love without jealousy.
There is no venom like that of the tongue.
There is a salve for every sore.
There's many a slip 'twixt the cup and the lip.
There's safety in numbers.
They who only seek for faults find nothing else.
Those who do nothing generally take to shouting.
Those who live in glass houses should not throw stones.
Those who make the best use of their time have none to spare.
Time and tide wait for no man.
Time cures more than the doctor.
Time flies.
Time is money.
Time is the best counsellor.
Tit for tat is fair play.
To be born with a silver spoon in the mouth.
To err is human; to forgive divine.
To forget a wrong is the best revenge.
To kill two birds with one stone.
To know the disease is half the cure.
To look for a needle in a haystack.
To make one hole to stop another.
To make two bites at one cherry.
To put the cart before the horse.
To scare a bird is not the best way to catch it.
To stir up a hornet's nest.
To take the chestnut out of the fire with the cat's paw.
Too many cooks spoil the broth.
Too much of one thing is good for nothing.
Train a tree when it is young.
Tread on a worm and it will turn.
True love never grows old.
True love never runs smoothly.
Trust but not too much.
Trust dies because bad pay poisons him.
Turn over a new leaf.
Two eyes see more than one.
Two heads are better than one.
Two is company, three is none.

Two is company, three is a crowd.

Two wrongs do not make a right.

Throw a sprat to catch a whale.

Undertake no more than you can perform.

Uneasy lies the head that wears a crown.

Union is strength.

Vice is its own punishment, virtue its own reward.

Walls have ears.

Wash your dirty linen at home.

Waste makes want.

Waste not, want not.

We are such stuff as dreams are made on.

We can live without our friends, but not without our neighbours.

Wedlock is like a place besieged; those within wish to get out, those
    without wish to get in.

Well begun is half done.

What belongs to everybody belongs to nobody.

What can't be cured must with patience be endured.

What cost nothing is worth nothing.

What's done can't be undone.

What is learnt in the cradle lasts to the tomb.

What is one man's meat is another man's poison.

What is sauce for the goose is sauce for the gander.

What is worth doing at all is worth doing well.

What man has done man can do.

Whatever you are be a man.

What the eye does not admire the heart does not desire.

What the eyes don't see the heart does not grieve for.

What the heart thinketh the tongue speaketh.

When a man is going down the hill everyone will give him a push.

When in Rome do as the Romans do.

When money's taken freedom's forsaken.

When poverty comes in at the door love flies out of the window.

When rogues fall out honest men come into their own.

When the cat is away the mice will play.

When the wine is in, the wit is out.

When thy neighbour's house doth burn, be careful of thine own.

When two friends have a common purse, one sings and the other weeps.

When wits meet sparks fly out.

Where ignorance is bliss, 'tis folly to be wise.
Where there is nothing to lose there is nothing to fear.
Where there is smoke there is fire.
Where there's a will there's a way.
While there is life there is hope.
While the grass grows the horse starves.
Who chatters to you will chatter of you.
Who judges others condemns himself.
Who knows most says least.
Who spends more than he should, shall not have to spend when he
     would.
Who will not hear must be made to feel.
Who will bell the cat?
Whom the gods love die young.
Wilful waste makes woeful want.
Wine and wenches empty men's purses.
Words are wind, but blows are unkind.
You cannot eat your cake and have it.
You cannot get blood out of a stone.
You cannot make a silk purse out of a sow's ear.
You cannot see the wood for the trees.
You cannot shoe a running horse.
You cannot teach old dogs new tricks.
You never know till you have tried.
Young men think old men fools; old men know young men to be so.
Youth and age will never agree.
Youth lives on hope, old age on remembrance.
Zeal without knowledge is a runaway horse.

100 CHOICE QUOTATIONS FOR SPECIAL OCCASIONS

Quotations are widely used by public speakers, teachers, scholars and businessmen. They come from some of the finest minds who have contributed to the richness of English and other languages. An apt quotation succinctly expresses a thought which would otherwise require many more words to convey the meaning adequately. In a book of this size the number of quotations must necessarily be restricted but they are choice ones. It is to be hoped that the users of *The Students' Companion* would be motivated to expand on this limited selection by their own research and further reading.

Absence
: The Lord watch between me and thee, when we are absent one from another. (The Bible. Genesis 31:49)

Achievement
: The heights by great men reached and kept
Were not attained by sudden flight;
But they, while their companions slept,
Were toiling upward in the night. (Longfellow)

Action
: All human activity is prompted by desire. (Bertrand Russell)
The only cure for grief is action. (G.H. Lewis)

Beauty
: A thing of beauty is a joy forever. (John Keats)

Belief
: The moment we want to believe something, we suddenly see all the arguments for it, and become blind to the arguments against it. (George Bernard Shaw)

Books
: Some books are to be tasted, others to be swallowed, and some to be chewed and digested. (Francis Bacon)
A good book is the precious life-blood of a master spirit. (John Milton)

Borrowing	Neither a borrower nor a lender be; For loan oft loses both itself and friend. (Shakespeare)
Charity	Our charity begins at home, and mostly ends where it begins. (Horace Smith)
Citizen	Healthy citizens are the greatest asset any country can have. (Sir Winston Churchill)
Commandment	Jesus said unto them: Thou shalt love the Lord Thy God with all thy heart, and with all thy soul, and with all thy mind. This is the first and great commandment. And the second is like unto it, Thou shalt love thy neighbour as thyself. (The Bible. St Matthew 22:37–39)
Contentment	Enjoy your own life without comparing it with that of another. (Condorcet)
Courtesy	The small courtesies sweeten life. (Bovee) Be courteous to all but intimate with few. (Washington)
Cowards	Cowards die many times before their deaths, The valiant never taste of death but once. (Shakespeare)
Deception	Things are seldom what they seem, Skim milk masquerades as cream. (W.S. Gilbert)
Death	In the midst of life we are in death. (Anglican Book of Common Prayer)
Defeat	Defeat should never be a source of discouragement but rather a fresh stimulus. (South)
Destiny	There is a divinity that shapes our ends, Rough hew them how we will. (Shakespeare)
Devil	The devil can cite scripture for his purpose. (Shakespeare)
Discretion	The better part of valour is discretion. (Shakespeare)

Distance   'Tis distance lends enchantment to the view.
              (Thomas Campbell)

Education   Education commences at the mother's knee, and
              every word spoken within the hearing of little
              children tends towards the formation of
              character. (Hosea Ballou)
              Education is the leading of human souls to what is
              best, and making what is best out of them.
              (John Ruskin)
              Our progress as a nation can be no swifter than our
              progress in education. The human mind is our
              fundamental resource. (John F. Kennedy)

Everything   Everything comes if a man will only wait. (Benjamin
              Disraeli)

Evil   The evil that men do lives after them;
              The good is oft interred with their bones.
              (Shakespeare)

Faith   Faith is to believe what we do not see. (St
              Augustine)
              All I have seen teaches me to trust the Creator for
              what I have not seen. (Emerson)

Fools   Fools rush in where angels fear to tread. (Pope)

Fortune   There is a tide in the affairs of men
              Which taken at the flood, leads on to fortune.
              (Shakespeare)

Freedom   Those who deny freedom to others deserve it not for
              themselves and under a just God cannot long
              retain it. (Abraham Lincoln)

Friends   There is nothing better than the encouragement of a
              good friend. (Katharine Hathaway)

Garden   One is nearer God's heart in a garden, than any-
              where else in the world. (Dorothy Gurney)
              God almighty first planted a garden, and indeed it is
              the purest of human pleasures. (Francis Bacon)

Genius   Genius is one percent inspiration and ninety-nine
              percent perspiration. (Edison)

God	God moves in a mysterious way His wonders to perform. (Cowper) With God all things are possible. (The Bible. St Mark 10:27) God is no respecter of persons. (The Bible. Acts 10:34)
Golden rule	As ye would that men should do to you, do ye also to them likewise. (The Bible. St Luke 6:31)
Grace	But grow in grace, and in the knowledge of our Lord and Saviour Jesus Christ. (The Bible. II Peter 3:18)
Greatness	Some are born great, some achieve greatness, and some have greatness thrust upon 'em. (Shakespeare)
Guest	The art of being a good guest is to know when to leave. (Prince Philip)
Habit	Habit, if not resisted, soon becomes necessity. (St Augustine)
Happiness	I have learned to seek happiness by limiting my desires rather than in attempting to satisfy them. (John Stuart Mill)
Heal	Heal me, O Lord, and I shall be healed; save me and I shall be saved. (The Bible. Jeremiah 17:14)
Home	Be it ever so humble, there's no place like home. (John H. Payne)
Hope	Hope is the only good which is common to all men. (Thales) Hoping and waiting is not my way of doing things. (Goethe)
Idleness	For Satan finds some mischief still for idle hands to do. (Isaac Watts)
Jealousy	He that is not jealous is not in love. (St Augustine)

Laughter   Laugh and the world laughs with you,
                Weep and you weep alone. (Ella Wheeler Wilcox)
                A good laugh is sunshine in a house. (Thackeray)

Learning   A little learning is a dangerous thing,
                Drink deep, or taste not the Pierian Spring:
                There shallow draughts intoxicate the brain,
                And drinking largely sobers us again. (Alexander
                    Pope)

Leisure   What is this life if, full of care,
                We have no time to stand and stare? (William H.
                Davies)

Liberty   Eternal vigilance is the price of liberty. (John P.
                    Curran)

Life   I expect to pass through this world but once. Any
                    good therefore that I can do or any kindness
                    that I can show to any fellow creatures, let me
                    do it now. (Anonymous)
                Life wouldn't be fun if it did not have its ups and
                    downs. (Mickey Rooney)
                Life is real; life is earnest.....
                Let us then be up and doing,
                With a heart for any fate,
                Still achieving, still pursuing,
                Learn to labour and to wait. (Longfellow)
                I am the bread of life: he that cometh to me shall
                    never hunger; and he that believeth in me shall
                    never thirst. (The Bible. Jesus: St John 6:35)

Light   Let your light so shine before men, that they may see
                    your good works, and glorify your Father which
                    is in heaven. (The Bible. St Matthew 5:16)

Love   The course of true love never did run smooth.
                    (Shakespeare)
                And thou shalt love the Lord with all thine heart,
                    and with all thy soul, and with all thy might.
                    (The Bible. Deuteronomy 6:5)

Man   God give us men. A time like this demands
                Strong minds, great hearts, true faith and ready
                    hands!

Men whom the lust of office does not kill,
Men whom the love of office cannot buy,
Men who possess opinions and a will,
Men who love honour, men who cannot lie.
   (J.G. Holland)

The attributes which a person should endeavour to cultivate to become well-rounded are so felicitously expressed in Rudyard Kipling's 'IF' that it has been quoted here almost in its entirety.

If you can keep your head when all about you
   Are losing theirs and blaming it on you,
If you can trust yourself when all men doubt you,
   But make allowance for their doubting too;
If you can wait and not be tired by waiting,
   Or being lied about, don't deal in lies,
Or being hated, don't give way to hating,
   And yet don't look too good, nor talk too wise:

If you can dream – and not make dreams your master;
   If you can think – and not make thoughts your aim;
If you can meet with Triumph and Disaster
   And treat those two imposters just the same.

If you can talk with crowds and keep your virtue,
   Or walk with kings nor lose the common touch,
If neither foes nor loving friends can hurt you,
   If all men count with you, but none too much;
If you can fill the unforgiving minute
   With sixty seconds worth of distance run,
Yours is the Earth and everything that's in it,
   And – which is more – you'll be a Man, my son. (Rudyard Kipling)

Whatsoever a man soweth, that shall he also reap. (The Bible. Galatians 6:7)

Money	For the love of money is the root of all evil. (The Bible. 1 Timothy 6:10)
Music	Music hath charms to soothe a savage breast. (William Congreve)
Name	Good name in man and woman, Is the immediate jewel of their souls. (Shakespeare) The purest treasure mortal times afford Is spotless reputation. (Shakespeare) A good name is rather to be chosen than great riches. (The Bible. Proverbs 22:1)
Nation	To your tender and loving hands the future of the nation is entrusted. In your innocent hearts the pride of the nation is enshrined. On your scholastic development the salvation of the nation is dependent. When you return to your classes after independence, remember therefore, each and every one of you, that you carry the future of Trinidad and Tobago in your school bags. (Dr Eric Williams, Prime Minister of Trinidad & Tobago. Message to the Youth of the Nation at Independence Youth Rally, 30th August, 1962.)
Obedience	To obey is better than sacrifice. (The Bible. 1 Samuel 15:22)
Patience	How poor are they that have not patience. What wound did ever heal but by degrees. (Shakespeare) What can't be cured, must (with patience) be endured. (Burton) Patience and perseverance overcome the greatest difficulties. (Clarissa)
Patriotism	Breathes there the man with soul so dead, Who never to himself hath said, This is my own, my native land. (William Scott)
Place	The eyes of the Lord are in every place, beholding the evil and the good. (The Bible. Proverbs 15:3)

Power	Power will intoxicate the best hearts, as wine the strongest heads. No man is wise enough, nor good enough to be trusted with unlimited power. (Charles Caleb Colton)
Praise	Let another man praise thee, and not thine own mouth. (The Bible. Proverbs 27:2)
Prayer	More things are wrought by prayer Than this world dreams of. (Tennyson)
Reading	Reading is to the mind what exercise is to the body. (Steele)
Season	To everything there is a season, and a time to every purpose under heaven. (The Bible. Ecclesiastes 3:1)
Shepherd	The Lord is my shepherd; I shall not want. (The Bible. Psalms 23:1)
Sin	Be sure your sin will find you out. (The Bible. Numbers 32:23)
Speech	I disapprove of what you say, but I will defend to the death your right to say it. (Voltaire)
Strength	My strength is as the strength of ten Because my heart is pure. (Tennyson)
Talk	Keep the golden mean between saying too much and too little. (Publillius Syrus)
Truth	Constantly speak the truth, boldly rebuke vice, and patiently suffer for the truth's sake. (Anglican Book of Common Prayer)
University	A University should be a place of light, of liberty and of learning. (Benjamin Disraeli)
Vision	Where there is no vision, the people perish. (The Bible. Proverbs 29:18)
Woman	A perfect woman, nobly planned, To warn, to comfort, and command. (Wordsworth)
Work	Light is the task when many share the toil. (Homer)

I never did anything worth doing by accident, nor did any of my inventions come by accident; they came by work. (Edison)

Incentives are what get people to work harder. (Nikita Kruschev)

World   It takes all sorts of people to make a world. (Douglas Jerrold)

Writing   The pen is mightier than the sword. (Edward Bulwer-Lytton)

If you wish to be a writer, write. (Epictetus)

Year   I said to the man who stood at the gate of the year:
'Give me a light that I may tread safely into the unknown.'
And he replied:
'Go out into the darkness and put your hand into the hand of God. That shall be to you better than light and safer than a known way.' (M.L. Haskins)

SMALL WORDS FOR BIG ONES

This section has been put into this book simply to provide mental recreation, and to help those who are interested in word games.

It is well to emphasise, however, that it is generally better to use the small rather than the big word, both in speaking and in writing.

Big word	Small word
cinerary	ashes
accessory	additional
contiguous	adjoining
derelict	abandoned
eschew	avoid
fortuitous	accidental
minauderie	affectation
pugnacious	aggressive
propitiate	appease
supercilious	arrogant
vituperate	abuse
factitious	artificial
plenipotentiary	ambassador
dudgeon	anger
cecity	blindness
jejune	bare
audacious	bold
sanguinary	blood-thirsty
encephalon	brain
thrasonical	boasting
decapitate, decollate	behead
impeccable	blameless
terminus	boundary
credence	belief
sterile	barren

Big word	Small word
insolvent	bankrupt
mendicant	beggar
salutary	beneficial
vaunt	boast
clocher	belfry
nigrescent	blackish
setaceous	bristly
vociferate	bawl
alacrity	briskness
osseous	bony
succinct	brief
turpitude	baseness
acerbity	bitterness
compendious	brief
pugilist	boxer
benediction	blessing
grandiloquent	bombastic
consuetude.	custom
recreant	coward
debonair	courteous
sangfroid	coolness, calmness
malediction	curse
puerile	childish
cupidity	covetousness
pellucid	clear

Big word	Small word
chanticleer	cock
felicitation	congratulation
perfunctory	careless
chronometer	clock
querimonious, querulous	complaining
vitiate	corrupt
calcareous	chalky
myriad	countless
coerce	compel
vanquish	conquer
insouciant	careless
acatalectic	complete
twaddle	chatter
obsequious	cringing
hamate	crooked
vouchsafe	condescend
ingenuous	candid
vicissitude	change
ludicrous	comical
frigid	cold
coagulation	clotting
masticate	chew
tranquil	calm
maladroit	clumsy
ambiguous, equivocal, dubious	doubtful
opprobrium	disgrace
beguile	deceive
ignominy	disgrace
desuetude	disuse
internecine	deadly
commination	denunciation
inebriate	drunk
labefaction	decay
procrastinate	defer
sediment	dregs
defeasance	defeat
denegation	denial
evanesce	disappear
insubordinate	disobedient
portal	door

Big word	Small word
traduce	defame
decadence	decay
lethal, lethiferous	deadly
quotidian	daily
demise	death
negation	denial
quiescent	dormant
assiduity	diligence
delectable	delightful
lexicon, thesaurus	dictionary
tenement	dwelling-house
hallucination	delusion
intrepidity	daring
aphonia	dumbness
prudence	discretion
esculent	edible
edible	eatable
avidity	eagerness
elucidate	explain
eximious	excellent
inane, vacuous	empty
sempervirent	evergreen
commutation	exchange
sempiternal	everlasting
tentative	experimental
adversary	enemy
exorbitant	excessive
oriental	eastern
reverberate	echo
interminable	endless
gratuitous	free
valediction	farewell
intimidate	frighten
obese	fat
quondam	former
adulation	flattery
parsimonious	frugal
absolution	forgiveness
plenary	full
plenitude	fullness
decrepit	feeble

Big word	Small word
oblivion	forgetfulness
timorous	fearful
aliment	food
inundate	flood
vapulation	flogging
prospicience	foresight
fatuous, desipient	foolish
prognosis	forecast
fugacious	fleeting
insipience	foolishness
plumose	feathery
sebacious, adipose	fatty
pusillanimous	faint-hearted
mendacity	falsehood
spurious	false
amity	friendship
fecundity	fruitfulness
replete	full
amicable	friendly
aptitude	fitness
edacious	greedy
hiatus	gap
mucilage	gum
cupidity	greed
vertigo	giddiness
confabulate	gossip
garish	gaudy
porraceous, viridescent	greenish
authentic	genuine
chivalrous	gallant
conjecture, surmise	guess
jocund	gay
habiliment	garment
culpable	guilty
voracious	gluttonous
gravamen	grievance
merchandise	goods
wraith	ghost
rapacious	greedy
callisthenics	gymnastics
domicile	house, home

Big word	Small word
gigantic	huge
ululate	howl
innocuous, innoxious	harmless
acephalous	headless
manacle	handcuff
assuetude	habit
co-adjutor	helper
pendulous	hanging
colossal	huge
recluse, anchorite	hermit
asperity	harshness
deleterious, noxious	hurtful
corneous	horny
animosity	hatred
cursory	hasty
nostalgia	home-sickness
secrete	hide
moiety	half
fainéant	idle
propensity	inclination
inadequate	insufficient
incarcerate	imprison
irascible	irritable
nescient	ignorant
simulacrum	image
animus	intention
valetudinarian	invalid
ameliorate	improve
afflatus	inspiration
contumelious	insolent
disingenuous	insincere
inexorable	inflexible
facetious	jocular
succulent	juicy
convivial	jovial
geniculate	knotted
osculate	kiss
erudite	learned
affirmation	oath

Big word	Small word
inanimate	lifeless
indolent, otiose	lazy
lascivious	lewd
deficiency	lack
missive	letter
vivacious	lively
amiable	lovable
delitescent	latent
munificent	liberal
clemency	leniency
salacious	lustful
effulgence	lustre
hilarious	merry
abstemious	moderate
banausic	mechanical
lugubrious	mournful
esoteric	mysterious
fallacious	misleading
labyrinth	maze
miscellaneous	mixed
alimony	maintenance
matrimony	marriage
venal	mercenary
deride	mock
mucedinous	mouldy
rabid	mad
hypochondriacal	melancholy
humidity	moisture
obstreperous, fremescent, boisterous	noisy
indigenous, vernacular	native
sobriquet	nickname
contiguity	nearness
adjacent	near
anonymous	nameless
proximity	nearness
oleaginous	oily
unguent	ointment
provenance	origin
umbrage	offence

Big word	Small word
avocation	occupation
elliptical	oval
extortionate	oppressive
translucent	opaque
senile	old
pristine	original
impecunious	penniless
encomium, eulogy	praise
impuissant	powerless
collateral	parallel
indigent	poor
calligraphy, chirography	penmanship
depurate	purify
aperient	purgative
tableau	picture
demotic	popular
peradventure	perhaps
commiseration	pity
lucrative	profitable
predatory	plundering
echinated	prickly
verisimilitude	probability
concierge	porter
hauteur	pride
prophylactic	preventive
copious	plentiful
petulant	peevish
defecate	purify
rapine	plunder
contaminate	pollute
orison	prayer
penitentiary	prison
enigma	puzzle
cantankerous	quarrelsome
charlatan	quack
expeditious	quick
conundrum	riddle
guerdon	reward
recapitulate	summarise

Big word	Small word
opulent, affluent	rich
taciturn	reserved
commodious	roomy, spacious
intermission	recess
recipient	receiver
udometer	rain-gauge
veritable	real
alacrity	readiness
temerarious	reckless
compunction	remorse
refescent	reddish
desultory	rambling
renovate	renew
insurgent	rebel
insurrection	rebellion
transgression	sin
vascid	sticky
arenaceous	sandy
deglutition	swallowing
espionage	spying
aspersion	slander
truculent	savage
velocity	swiftness
disseminate	scatter
somnolence	sleep
edulcorate	sweeten
expectorate	spit
lentitude	slowness
pertinacious	stubborn
acauline	stemless
proclivitous	steep
homily	sermon
consign	send
exiguous	small
obdurate	stubborn
surreptitious, clandestine	secret
acerbity	sourness
interstice	space
prehensile	seizing
declivity	slope
pishogue	sorcery
amanuensis	secretary

Big word	Small word
celerity	swiftness
surveillance	supervision
firmament	sky
intimidate	scare
emolument	salary
sedentary	sitting
fortitude	strength
contumacious	stubborn
sudation	sweat
amorphous	shapeless
insomnia	sleeplessness
subaltern	subordinate
immaculate	spotless
asphyxia	suffocating
tardy	slow
conspectus	synopsis
reticent	silent
succedaneum	substitute
taciturn	silent
vilify	slander
garrulous, loquacious	talkative
cogitate	think
depredator	thief
totile	twisted
endeavour	try
lacerate, lancinate	tear
veracity	truth
minacious	threatening
sepulchre	tomb
titillate	tickle
anourous	tailless
stratagem	trick
tenuity	thinness
chicanery	trickery
diaphanous	transparent
edentate	toothless
histrionic	theatrical
pedagogue	teacher
consentaneous	unanimous
incertitude	uncertainty
incessant	unceasing

Big word	Small word	Big word	Small word
oecumenical	universal	undulate	wavy
rectitude	uprightness	lassitude	weariness
ineffable	unspeakable	oscillate, vacillate	waver
mendacious	untruthful	debility	weakness
subterranean	underground	mundane	worldly
coalesce	unite	affluence	wealthy
micturate	urinate	decrescent	waning
infallible	unerring	nefarious	wicked
inquietude	uneasiness	textile	woven
		erroneous	wrong
furlough	vacation	delinquent	wrong-doer
quixotic	visionary	occidental	western
regurgitate	vomit	hebdomadal	weekly
effeminate	womanish	juvenescence	youthfulness
condign	worthy		

COMPARISONS OR SIMILES

as active as quicksilver.
as afraid as a grasshopper.
as ageless as the sun.
as agile as a cat—a monkey.
as alert as a chamois—as a bird in springtime.
as alike as two peas.
as alone as a leper—as Crusoe.
as ambitious as the devil—as Lady Macbeth.
as ancient as the sun—as the stars.
as angry as a wasp.
as far apart as the poles.
as arid as the sands of Sahara.
as artificial as clockwork—as made ice.
as audacious as the day.
as awful as justice—as thunder—as silence.
as awkward as a cow on ice.

as bad as the itch—as a blight.
as bald as a coot—as a billiard ball—as an egg.
as bare as a stone—as winter.
as barren as winter rain.
as bashful as a schoolgirl.
as beautiful as the sunset—as the rainbow.
as big as an elephant—as a whale.
as bitter as hemlock—as wormwood—as gall.
as black as ebony.
as blameless as the snow.
as blank as an empty bottle.
as blind as a bat—as ignorance.
as blithe as May.
as blue as indigo—as forget-me-nots.

as blunt as a hammer—as the back of a knife.
as boisterous as stormy sea winds.
as bold as brass—as a lion.
as boundless as the ocean.
as bounteous as nature.
as brainless as a chimpanzee.
as brave as Achilles.
as brief as time—as a dream.
as bright as a new penny—as a new shilling—as bright as a button.
as brilliant as a mirror—as stars.
as brisk as a flea—as a bailiff.
as brittle as glass.
as broad as Heaven's expanse.
as brown as a berry—as a bun—as hazelnuts.
as buoyant as wings.

as calm as a summer sea—as glass—as death.
as candid as mirrors.
as careless as the wind.
as cautious as a fox—as a Scot.
as certain as the rising of the morning sun—as Christmas.
as changeable as the moons.
as chaste as Minerva—as a lily.
as cheap as dirt—as lies.
as cheeky as a young bantam cock.
as cheerful as the birds—as the day was long.
as cheerless as the grave.
as cheery as a sunbeam.
as chill as death—as chilly as a tomb.
as chubby as a cherub.
as clammy as death.
as clean as a Dutch oven—as a new pin.
as clear as daylight—as crystal—as a bell—as rock water.
as clever as paint.
as clumsy as a bear.
as coarse as hemp—as fustian.
as cold as a dog's nose—as cold as a frog—as cold as a corpse.
as comfortable as coin.
as common as pins—as common as poverty—as dirt.

as complacent as a cat.
as confident as Hercules—as justice.
as conscientious as a dog.
as consoling as night.
as constant as the sun.
as contagious as a yawn.
as contrary as light and dark.
as convincing as the multiplication table.
as cool as a cucumber.
as costly as an election.
as cosy as the nest of a bird.
as countless as the stars—as hairs—as the desert sands.
as cowardly as a wild duck.
as crafty as a fox.
as credulous as a child.
as crisp as new bank notes.
as crooked as a corkscrew.
as cruel as Media—as winter—as death.
as cunning as a fox—as a monkey.
as curious as a fish.

as dangerous as machine-guns.
as dark as a dungeon—as pitch—as midnight.
as dead as a doornail—as the Roman Empire—as wood—as mutton.
as deaf as a beetle—as the billows.
as deceitful as the devil.
as deceptive as the mirage of the desert.
as deep as despair—as hell—as the sea.
as dejected as a wet hen.
as delicious as forbidden fruit—as a dream.
as desolate as a tomb.
as devoted as a faithful dog.
as difficult as a Greek puzzle—as a beginning.
as dirty as a hog.
as disappointing as wet gunpowder.
as dismal as a hearse.
as distant as the horizon.
as dizzy as a goose.
as docile as a lamb.

as dreadful as a gathering storm.
as dreary as an Asian steppe—as an empty house.
as drunk as a top—as fish—as a beggar.
as dry as dust—as a bone.
as dull as ditch water—as lead.
as dumb as an oyster—as a mouse.

as eager as a bridegroom.
as easy as pie—as shelling peas—as lying.
as elastic as a caterpillar.
as eloquent as Cicero.
as elusive as quicksilver.
as empty as an idiot's mind—as space.
as enticing as a riddle.
as essential as the dew.
as expensive as glory.

as fabulous as Aladdin's ring.
as faint as the hum of distant bees.
as fair as the morn—as truth—as Eve in Paradise.
as faithful as the dog—as the sun.
as faithful as fair weather.
as false as dice.
as familiar as an oath—as a popular song.
as far as the poles asunder.
as fast as light—as an eagle—as a storm.
as fat as a porpoise—a sheep's tail—as a distillery pig.
as fickle as the weather—as friends—as the sea.
as fidgety as an old maid.
as fierce as a famished wolf—as wolves.
as firm as faith—as adamant—as rocky mountains—as steel.
as fit as a fiddle.
as fixed as the laws of the Medes and the Persians—as fate.
as flabby as a sponge.
as flat as a pancake—as flat as the fens of Holland.
as fleet as a greyhound—as the wind.
as flimsy as gauze—as gossamer.
as foolish as a calf.

as foul as slander—as a sty.
as frail as a lily—as flowers—as glass.
as free as a breeze—as thought—as a fly.
as fresh as dew—as a sea breeze—as a rose.
as friendless as an alarm clock.
as friendly as a puppy.
as frigid as an iceberg.
as frightened as Macbeth before the ghost of Banquo.
as frisky as a colt.
as frizzled as a lawyer's wig.
as fruitful as Egypt.
as full as an egg is of meat.

as game as a fighting cock.
as garrulous as a magpie—as an old maid.
as gaudy as a butterfly.
as gay as a bullfinch—as larks—as the spring.
as generous as a dream—as a lord.
as genial as sunshine.
as gentle as a fawn—as a turtle dove—as sleep—as falling dew.
as glad as a fly—as a blooming tree.
as glib as glass.
as glossy as a mole—as the finest silk.
as gloomy as night.
as glorious as the sun.
as glum as an oyster—as mud.
as gluttonous as curiosity.
as good as gold—as a play.
as gorgeous as a Sultana—as the Heavens.
as graceful as a fawn.
as gracious as the morn—as a duchess.
as grand as a victory—as a Greek statue—as the world.
as grave as a judge.
as grey as time—as smoke.
as great as a lord.
as greedy as a hog—as a cormorant.
as green as grass—as a leaf.
as grim as death—as hell.

as haggard as spectres.
as hairless as an egg.
as hairy as a mastodon—a spider.
as handsome as paint.
as happy as a lark—as a child—as a lord.
as hard as flint—as granite—as steel.
as harmless as a babe.
as harsh as truth—as a grating wheel.
as hasty as fire.
as hateful as death—as hateful as hell.
as haughty as the devil.
as healthy as a May morning.
as hearty as an oak.
as heavy as lead.
as helpless as a babe.
as hideous as the witch of Endor.
as high as Heaven—as the stars.
as hoarse as a raven.
as hollow as a drum.
as honest as a mirror.
as hopeful as the break of day.
as horny as a camel's knee.
as horrid as a murderer's dream.
as hot as pepper—as hell—as fire—as molten lead.
as hueless as a ghost.
as huge as high Olympus.
as humble as a worm—as Uriah Heep.
as hungry as a wolf—as a bear—as the grave—as a church mouse.
as hushed as midnight.

as ignorant as a child.
as illimitable as the boundless sea.
as illusive as a dream.
as immaculate as an angel.
as immense as the sea.
as immortal as the stars.
as immutable as the laws of the Medes and the Persians.
as impatient as a lover.
as imperishable as eternity.

as impetuous as a poet.
as inconsistent as the moon—as the waves.
as indolent as an old bachelor.
as industrious as an ant.
as inevitable as death.
as inexhaustible as the deep sea.
as inexorable as the grave.
as inflexible as a granite rock.
as innocent as a lamb—as a babe.
as invisible as the air.

as jealous as a Spaniard—as a cat.
as jolly as a shoe brush.
as joyful as a fly.
as joyous as the laughter of a child.
as jubilant as old sleigh bells.

as keen as a razor—as hunger—as mustard.
as killing as a plague.
as kind as consent.
as knowing as the stars.

as languid as a love-sick maid.
as lasting as the pyramids.
as lawful as eating.
as lawless as the stormy wind.
as lax as cut string.
as lazy as a toad—as a lobster—as a ship in the doldrums.
as lean as Sancho's ass—as a lath—as a skeleton.
as level as a pond.
as liberal as the sun.
as lifeless as the grave.
as light as down—as air—as cork—as a feather.
as lithe as a panther—as a tiger.
as little as Tom Thumb—as a squirrel.
as lively as a cricket.
as loathsome as a toad.
as lonely as a deserted ship—as the Arctic Sea.
as loquacious as Polonious.

as loud as thunder—as a horn.
as lovely as Venus—as the violet.
as low as the grave.
as lowly as a slave.
as loyal as a dove.

as mad as a hatter—as a March hare.
as magnanimous as Agamemnon.
as malicious as Satan.
as mean as a miser.
as meek as a dove—as a mouse.
as merciless as the grave—as Othello—as ambition.
as merry as a lark.
as merry as spring.
as mild as a dove—as moonlight.
as mischievous as a kitten—as a monkey.
as mobile as humanity.
as modest as a dove—as a primrose.
as monotonous as the sea.
as motionless as a corpse.
as mournful as the grave.
as muddy as sheep dogs.
as mum as an oyster.
as mute as the tomb—as the grave.
as mysterious as an echo—as a sphinx.

as naked as night—as a peeled apple.
as natural as life.
as nearsighted as a mole.
as neat as a nail—as ninepins.
as needful as the sun.
as nervous as a mouse.
as new as day.
as nice as ninepence.
as nimble as a lizard—as quicksilver.
as noiseless as a shadow.
as noisy as a menagerie.
as numerous as the sands upon the ocean shore.

as obedient as a puppet—as the scabbard.
as obnoxious as an alligator.
as obstinate as a mule—as a pig.
as old as creation—as Methuselah—as Trilobites.
as opaque as the sky.
as open as a smile.
as opposite as the poles.

as pale as Banquo's ghost—as death.
as passionate as young love.
as patient as the hours—as Job.
as peaceful as sleep.
as persistent as a mosquito.
as piercing as light.
as placid as a duck-pond.
as plain as a pikestaff.
as playful as a rabbit—as kittens.
as pleasant as health.
as pleased as Punch.
as plentiful as blackberries.
as poor as a church mouse—as Job.
as populous as an ant hill.
as powerful as death—as a lion.
as powerless as an infant.
as pretty as a picture—as paint.
as progressive as time.
as proud as a peacock—as Lucifer.
as punctual as springtime.
as pure as a lily—as winter snow—as faith.

as quarrelsome as the weasel.
as quick as a flash—as quick as thought.
as quiet as a mouse—as a lamb.

as ragged as Lazarus.
as rapid as lightning.
as rare as a blue rose—as rare as a comet.
as ravenous as a winter wolf.

as real as the stars.
as rebellious as the sea.
as red as a cherry—as blood—as a poppy.
as regal as Juno.
as regular as sunrise.
as relentless as fate.
as remote as a dream.
as resistless as the wind.
as restless as ambition—as the sea.
as rich as Croesus—as a Creole.
as rosy as a bride—as the morn.
as rotten as dirt.
as rough as hemp—as a storm.
as round as the O of Giotto.
as rude as a bear.
as rugged as a rhinoceros.
as ruthless as the sea.

as sacred as a shrine.
as sad as night—as doom.
as safe as a tortoise under its shell—a sardine.
as salt as a sea sponge—as brine.
as saucy as the wave.
as scarce as hen's teeth—as feathers on a fish.
as secret as thought.
as secure as the grave.
as seedy as a raspberry.
as selfish as a fox.
as senseless as stones.
as sensitive as a flower.
as serious as a doctor—as an owl.
as shallow as a pan.
as shameful as a sin.
as shameless as a nude statue.
as shapeless as an old shoe.
as sharp as a razor—as a thistle.
as short as any dream—as the life of a wave.
as shy as the squirrel—as the fawn.
as sick as a dog.

as silent as thought—as a stone.
as silly as calves.
as simple as A.B.C.—as a child.
as sincere as sunlight.
as sleek as a mouse.
as sleepless as owls.
as slippery as ice—as a serpent.
as slow as a snail.
as sly as a fox.
as small as atoms.
as smart as a sixpence—as paint.
as smooth as ice.
as sober as a judge.
as soft as wool—as velvet—as fur—as silk.
as solid as bricks.
as solitary as a tomb.
as soothing as the breath of Spring.
as sour as lime.
as spacious as the element.
as speechless as a stone.
as spineless as a jelly-fish.
as spiteful as a monkey.
as spotless as snow—as lilies.
as spruce as an onion.
as stale as old beer.
as stately as an oak—as a queen.
as steadfast as the sun.
as stealthy as a cat.
as stiff as a stone—as a ramrod.
as still as a log—as a statue.
as stinking as a polecat—as carrion.
as straight as a candle—as a lance.
as strange as a vision.
as strong as Hercules—as brandy—as Samson.
as stubborn as a mule.
as stupid as a sloth—as a log—as a post.
as subtle as a serpent.
as sudden as a snap—as lightning.
as sulky as a bear.

as superfluous as a fifth wheel.
as superstitious as sailors.
as supple as a snake.
as sure as a gun—as sunrise—as death.
as suspicious as a cat.
as sweet as a rose—as sugar.
as swift as an arrow—as lightning—as a flash—as thought.

as talkative as a magpie.
as tall as a steeple.
as tame as a sheep.
as taut as a fiddle string.
as tedious as a guilty conscience.
as tender as a bud—as a lamb—as tears.
as terrible as Jove—as hell.
as thick as ants—as thieves—as hail.
as thin as a wafer—as a groat—as a lath.
as thirsty as a sponge—as Tantalus.
as thoughtless as a lark.
as tidy as a candy shop.
as tight as a drum head—as teeth.
as timid as a mouse—as a fawn.
as tired as tombstones.
as tough as leather—as nails.
as trackless as the sea—as the desert.
as tranquil as the summer sea.
as transient as lightning.
as transparent as glass.
as treacherous as the memory.
as tricky as an ape.
as trivial as a parrot's prate.
as troublesome as a monkey.
as true as the gospel—true as steel.
as truthful as a knight of old.
as tuneless as a bag of wool.

as ugly as a scarecrow—as sin—as a bear.
as unapproachable as a star.
as unattractive as a gargoyle.

as uncertain as the weather.
as unchangeable as the past.
as unclean as sin.
as uncomplaining as a lamb.
as uncompromising as justice.
as unconquerable as chewing gum.
as uncontrollable as the wave.
as unfeeling as rocks.
as unhappy as King Lear.
as universal as seasickness—as light.
as unmerciful as the billows.
as unprofitable as smoke.
as unreal as a dream.
as unstable as the wind.
as unsteady as the ocean.
as unusual as a sailor on horseback.
as upright as a tower.
as useful as a cow.

as vague as a shadow—as futurity.
as vain as a peacock.
as various as the weather—as variable as the weather.
as vast as eternity.
as venomous as a snake.
as vigilant as the stars.
as vigorous as fire.
as violent as steam.
as virtuous as holy truth.
as voiceless as the tomb.
as voracious as a camel.
as vulgar as money.

as wan as moonlight—as ashes.
as warlike as the wolf.
as warm as sunbeams—as wool.
as wary as a fox.
as wasteful as a hen.
as watchful as a sentinel.
as wavering as Hamlet.

as weak as water—as a reed.
as weather-beaten as a fisherman's oar.
as welcome as dew on parched flowers.
as welcome as a rainstorm in hell—as a star.
as wet as a fish—as a drowned rat.
as white as porcelain—as snow—as fleece—as ivory—as a lily.
as wide as hope.
as wilful as a mule.
as wily as a fox.
as wise as Solomon.
as witless as a jackdaw.

as yellow as saffron—as jaundice—as sulphur.
as young as morn—as dawn.
as youthful as the month of May.

as zigzag as lightning.

ABBREVIATIONS IN COMMON USE

Generally abbreviations which can be pronounced as a word, e.g. NATO do not have full stops between the letters; abbreviations which end with the last letter of the full word also do not have a full stop. Otherwise full stops are usually used. No full stops are used with abbreviations of metric units.

A1 . . . . First Class
A.A. . . . . . Automobile Association; Anti-Aircraft
A.A.A. . . . . Amateur Athletic Association
A.B. . . . . Able-bodied seaman
abbr. . . . . .abbreviation
a/c . . . . account
A.C.P. . . . . Associate of the College of Preceptors
A.D. . . . . (*Anno Domini*) In the year of Our Lord
ad. . . . . .advertisement
A.D.C. . . . . aide-de-camp
ad lib. . . . . . (*ad libitum*) as much as you like
A.E.C. . . Army Educational Corps
A.E.F. . . Allied Expeditionary Force
A.I.Mech.E. . . . . . Associate of the Institute of Mechanical Engineers
a.m. . . (*ante meridiem*) before noon
A.M. . . . . amplitude modulated
A.M.I.C.E. . . Associate Member of the Institute of Civil Engineers
anon. . . . . anonymous
A.N.Z.A.C. . . . Australian and New Zealand Army Corps
A.R.C.M. . . Associate of the Royal College of Music

A.R.P. . . . . . Air Raid Precautions
Assn . . . . Association
Asst . . . . Assistant
Att.-Gen. . . . . . . Attorney-General
A.V. . . . . . . Authorised Version (of the Bible)

B.A. . . . . .Bachelor of Arts
Bart . . . . Baronet
B.B.C. . . British Broadcasting Corp.
B.C. . . . . Before Christ
B. Comm. . . Bachelor of Commerce
B.D. . . . . Bachelor of Divinity
B.E.F. . . . . . . British Expeditionary Force
B.M.A. . . . . British Medical Association
B.R.C.S. . . . . . . .British Red Cross Society
Brit. . . . . Britain; British; Britannia
B.Sc. . . . . Bachelor of Science
B.Sc.(Econ.). . . Bachelor of Science, Economics
B.S.T. . . . . . . British Summer Time
Bt . . . . .Baronet; bought
B.Th. . . . . . . Bachelor of Theology
B.W.I. . . . . British West Indies

B.W.I.A. . . . . . British West Indian Airways
© . . . . copyright
C . . . . Centigrade
C.A. . . . . . . .Chartered Accountant
C.A.N.A. Caribbean News Agency
Cantab. . . . . of Cambridge (University)
cap. . . . . capital letter; chapter
Capt. . . . . Captain
Caricom . . . Caribbean Community
Carifesta . . . . . . Carribean Festival of the Arts
CARIFTA . . . . Caribbean Free Trade Area
C.B. . . . . .Companion of the Order of the Bath
C.B.E. . . . .Companion of the Order of the British Empire
C.C. . . . . County Council
cc (or cm³). . . . . . cubic centimetre
C.C.C. . . . . Caribbean Council of Churches
C.D.B. . . . Caribbean Development Bank
C.E. . . . . Civil Engineer
cf. . . . . compare
C.G.M. . . . . Conspicuous Gallantry Medal
C.H. . . . . . .Companion of Honour
C.I.A. . .Central Intelligence Agency
C.I.D. . . . . . Criminal Investigation Department
CIDA . . . . . Canadian International Development Agency
c.i.f. . . . . . . cost, insurance, freight
cm . . . . centimetre
cm² . . . . square centimetre
cm³ . . . . cubic centimetre
C.M.G. . . . Companion of the Order of St Michael and St George
C.M.S. . . . . . . .Church Missionary Society

Co. . . . . Company
c/o . . . . .care of
C.O.D. . . . . Cash on Delivery
Corp. . . . . .Corporation
C. of E. . . . . . .Church of England
Col . . . . Colonel
Cpl . . . . Corporal
C.P.R. . . Canadian Pacific Railway
Cr. . . . . credit, creditor
C.S. . . . . .Civil Service
C.V.O. . . Commander of the Royal Victorian Order
cwt . . . . hundredweight
C.X.C. . . .Caribbean Examinations Council

D.B.E. . . Dame Commander of the Order of the British Empire
D.D. . . . . Doctor of Divinity
deg. . . . . degree
Dept. . . . . Department
Deut. . . . . .Deuteronomy
D.F.C. . Distinguished Flying Cross
diam. . . . . diameter
dim. . . . . diminutive
D.Lit. . . . . . . .Doctor of Literature
D.Litt. . . . . Doctor of Letters
do. . . . . ditto, the same
doz. . . . . dozen
D.P.H. . . . . . Department of Public Health; Diploma in Public Health
Dr. . . . . .Doctor; debtor
D.S.C. . .Distinguished Service Cross
D.Sc. . . . . Doctor of Science
D.S.M. . . . . . Distinguished Service Medal
D.S.O. . . . . . Distinguished Service Order
D.Th. . . . . Doctor of Theology
D.V. . . . . (*Deo volente*) God willing

ea. . . . . each
E.C.C.M. . . . . . . Eastern Caribbean Common Market

E.C.L.A. . . Economic Commission for Latin America

ECOWAS . . Economic Community of West African States

EEC . . . . European Economic Community

EFTA . . . . . . European Free Trade Association

E. & O.E. . . . Errors and omissions excepted

e.g. . . .(*exemplie gratia*) for example

E.R. . . . .(*Elizabeth Regina*) Queen Elizabeth

esp. . . . . especially

Esq. . . . . Esquire

etc. . . . . (*et cetera*) and so forth

et seq. . . . . (*et sequens*) and the following

ex. . . . . .example

exp. . . . . export

F. . . . . .Fahrenheit

F.A.O. . . . . . Food and Agriculture Organisation

F.B.I. . . . . Federal Bureau of Investigation

fcap., fcp. . . . . .foolscap

Fid. Def. (*Fidei Defensor*) . Defender of the Faith

fig. . . . . figure; figurative

fin. . . . . at the end

FM . . . . frequency modulated

f.o.b. . . . . .free on board

fol., foll. . . . . following

fr. franc

F.R.A.M. . . . . Fellow of the Royal Academy of Music

F.R.C.P. . . . . . Fellow of the Royal College of Physicians

F.R.C.S. . . . . . Fellow of the Royal College of Surgeons

F.R.G.S. . . . . . Fellow of the Royal Geographical Society

F.R.H.S. . . . . . Fellow of the Royal Horticultural Society

F.R.Hist.S. . . . Fellow of the Royal Historical Society

g. . . . . .gram

GATT. . . . . . . .General Agreement on Tariffs and Trade

G.B.E. . . . . .(Knight) Grand Cross of the Order of the British Empire

G.C.F. . . . .greatest common factor

G.C.M. . . greatest common measure

G.C.M.G. . . .(Knight) Grand Cross of the Order of St Michael and St George

G.D.P. . . . Gross Domestic Product

G.G. . . . . Governor General

G.M. . . . . George Medal

G.M.T. . . . . Greenwich Mean Time

G.N.P. . . . Gross National Product

Govt . . . . .Government

G.P.O. . . . . . . .General Post Office

ha. . . . . hectare

H.C.F. . . . . highest common factor

H.I.S. . . . .(*hic iacet sepultus*) here lies buried

H.M. . . . . . . His (or Her) Majesty

H.M.S. . . . . His (or Her) Majesty's Ship or Service

Hon. . . . . . . Honourable; Honorary

h.p. . . . . .horse power

H.R.H. . . . . . . .His (or Her) Royal Highness

ib., ibid . . (*ibidem*) in the same place

ICBM . . . . .inter-continental ballistic missile

I.C.E. . . . . .Institute of Civil Engineers

id. . . . . (*idem*) the same

I.D.B. . . . . Inter-American Development Bank

I.A.T.A. . . . . International Air Transport Association

i.e. . . . . (*id est*) that is

I.E.E. . . . . . . Institute of Electrical Engineers

IHS. . . . . Jesus

I.L.P. . . Independent Labour Party

IMF . . International Monetary Fund

infra dig . . . . (*infra dignitatem*) beneath one's dignity

I.N.R.I. . . . . Jesus of Nazareth King of the Jews

inst . . . . . instant, the present month

I.O.C. . . . . . . International Olympic Committee

I.O.U. . . . . I owe you

jnr, jr . . . . junior

J.P. . . . . Justice of the Peace

K.C.B. . Knight Commander of the Order of the Bath

K.C.M.G. . . Knight Commander of the Order of St. Michael and St. George

kg . . . . kilogram

K.G.B. . . . . . . Soviet Secret Police

km . . . . kilometre

Kt. . . . . Knight

Kt. Bach. . . . . Knight Bachelor

kw . . . . kilowatt (1000 watts)

l . . . . litre

Lab. . . . . Labour; laboratory

Lat. . . . . Latin; latitude

lb. pound

l.b.w. . . . leg before wicket (cricket)

L.C.M. . . . lowest common multiple

L.C.P. . . . . Licentiate of the College of Preceptors

L.-Cpl . . . . Lance-Corporal

L.D.C. . . . Less Developed Country

L.D.S. . Licentiate of Dental Surgery

Lieut., or Lt. . . . . Lieutenant

LL.B . . . . Bachelor of Laws

LL.D. . . . . Doctor of Laws

log. . . . . logarithm

long. . . . . longitude

L.R.C.P. . . . Licentiate of the Royal College of Physicians

Lt.-Col . . . . Lieutenant-Colonel

Ltd . . . . Limited

m . . . . metre

m² . . . . square metre

m³ . . . . cubic metre

M.A. . . . . Master of Arts

M.B.E. . . . . . Member of the Order of the British Empire

M.C. . . . . Military Cross

M.D. . . . . Doctor of Medicine

M.D.C. . More Developed Country

Messrs . . . . Gentlemen

mfg . . . . manufacturing

M.H.R. . . . . . Member of the House of Representatives

M.L.C. . . Member of the Legislative Council

mm . . . . . . millimetre or millimetres

Mme . . . . Madame

M.O. . . . . Money Order

M.O.H. . . Medical Officer of Health

M.P. . . . . . . Member of Parliament

Mr . . . . Mister

M.R.C.P. . . . . Member of the Royal College of Physicians

Mrs . Mistress (pronounced Missis)

MS . . . . Manuscript

MSS . . . . Manuscripts

Mt. . . . . Mountain

M.V.O. . . . . . Member of the Royal Victorian Order

NATO. . . . . . North Atlantic Treaty Organisation

naut. . . . . nautical

N.B. . . . . (*nota bene*) note well

N.C.O. . . . . Non-commissioned Officer

neg. . . . . negative

nem. con. . . . . no-one contradicting

No. . . . . number

nol. pros. . . . . . . to be unwilling to prosecute

non seq. . . . . it does not follow

N.U.T. . . . . National Union of Teachers

o/a . . . . on account

O.A.S. . . . . Organisation of American States

O.A.U. . . . . Organisation of African Unity

o.b. . . . . (he, or she) died

O.B.E. . . . . Officer of the Order of the British Empire

O.M. . . . . Order of Merit

O.P. . . . . out of print

OPEC . . Organisation of Petroleum Exporting Countries

O.T. . . . . Old Testament

Oxon. . . . . . of Oxford (University)

oz. . . . . ounce

pd. . . . . paid

per cent. . . . . by the hundred

Ph.B. . . . . . Bachelor of Philosophy

Ph.D. . . . . . . Doctor of Philosophy

p.m. . . . . (*post meridiem*) afternoon

P.M. . . . . Prime Minister

P.M.G. . . . . . . Postmaster-General

pos. . . . . positive

Pres. . . . . President

pro . . . . professional

pro tem. . . . . for the time being

prox. . . . . (*proximo*) next month

P.S. . . . . . (postscript) written after

P.T. . . . . Pupil Teacher; Physical Training

Pte . . . . Private

P.T.O. . . . . Please turn over

P.W.D. . . Public Works Department

Q.C. . . . . Queen's Counsel

q.e.d. . . (*quod erat demonstrandum*) which was to be proved

q.e.f. . . . . (*quod erat faciendum*) which was to be done

qr. . . . . quarter

q.t. . . . . quart

q.v. . . . . (*quod vide*) which see

R.A. . . . . Royal Artillery; Royal Academy (of Art)

R.A.F. . . . . Royal Air Force

R.A.M. . . Royal Academy of Music

R.A.M.C. . . . Royal Army Medical Corps

R.C. . . . . Roman Catholic

R.C.S. . . Royal College of Surgeons

R.D. . . . . Rural Dean

Rd . . . . Road

re., ref. . . . . reference

Rev. . . . . Reverend

R.H.S. . Royal Horticultural Society

R.I.P. . . . . (*Requiescat in pace*) may he, or she, rest in peace

R.M.C. . . . . Royal Military College

R.N. . . . . Royal Navy

R.N.A.S. . . Royal Naval Air Service

R.N.R. . . . . . Royal Naval Reserve

R.N.V.R. . . Royal Naval Volunteer Reserve

r.p.m. . . . . . revolutions per minute

R.S.P.C.A. . . Royal Society for the Prevention of Cruelty to Animals

R.S.V.P. . . (*Répondez s'il vous plait*) Please reply

Rt. Hon. . . . . . . Right Honourable

R.T.S. . . . . . Religious Tract Society

Sec. . . . . Secretary

seq. . . . . the following
Sgt . . . . Sergeant
S.O.S. . . . . "Save our Souls"
(a signal of distress)
sov. . . . . sovereign
S.P.C.K. . . . . Society for the
Promotion of Christian
Knowledge
S.P.G. . . . . Society for the
Propagation of the Gospel
sq. . . . . square
S.R.N. . . . . State Registered Nurse
S.S. . . . . Steamship
St . . . . Saint, or street
Supt . . . . Superintendent
T.N.T. . . . . Trinitrotoluene
(an explosive)
Treas. . . . . Treasurer
T.U.C. . . . Trades Union Congress

U.D.C. . . . . Urban District Council
U.F.C. . . . . . . United Free Church
U.F.O. . Unidentified Flying Object
U.H.F. . . . . . Ultra high frequency
U.K. . . . . United Kingdom
ult. . . . . (*ultimo*) last month
UNESCO . . . . United Nations
Educational Scientific and
Cultural Organisation
U.N. . . . . United Nations
Unctad . . . . United Nations
Commission for Trade
and Development
U.N.D.P. . . . . United Nations
Development Programme
UNDRO . . United Nations Disaster
Relief Organisation
UNICEF . . . . United Nations
International Children's
Emergency Fund
UNIDO . . . . United Nations
Industrial Development
Organisation

UNRWA. . . . United Nations Relief
and Works Agency
UNO . . . . United Nations
Organisation
UNRRA . . . . United Nations
Relief and Rehabilitation
Administration
U.S.A. . . United States of America
USAID. . . . . United States Agency
for International Development
U.S.S. . . . . United States Ship
U.S.S.R. . . Union of Soviet Socialist
Republics
U.W.I.. . . . . University of the
West Indies

V.A.D. . Voluntary Aid Detachment
V.C. . . . . Victoria Cross
V.D. . . . . Venereal Disease
Ven. . . . . Venerable
verb. sap. . . . . (*verbum sapienti*)
A word is enough for a
wise man
V.G. . . . . Vicar General
V.H.F. . . . . . . very high frequency
via . . . . by way of
viz. . . . . (*videlicet*) namely
V.S.,(Vet.) . . . . . Veterinary Surgeon

W.H.O. . . . . World Health
Organisation
W.R.A.C. . . Women's Royal Army
Corps
W.D. . . . . War Department
W.R.A.F. . . . . Women's Royal
Air Force
W.R.I. . . . Women's Rural Institute
W.R.N.S. . . . . Women's Royal
Naval Service
W.S. . . . . Writer to the Signet
W.V.S. . . . . . . Women's Voluntary
Service

Xmas . . . . Christmas

Y.M.C.A. . . Young Men's Christian Association

yr . . . . younger, year

Y.W.C.A. . . . . . . Young Women's Christian Association

PREFIXES IN COMMON USE

ab, abs, a-   away from: e.g. abnormal, avert, abstract.

ad, (a, ac, af, ag, al, an, ap, ar, as, at)-   to: e.g. adjoin, ascend, accede, affix, aggravate, alleviate, annex, append, arrive, assimilate, attain.

ambi, amphi-   both: e.g. ambidexterous, amphibian, amphibious.

ante-   before: antecedent, antediluvian, anticipate.

anti-   against: e.g. antidote, antipathy, anti-aircraft, antiseptic.

arch-   leader, chief: e.g. archangel, archbishop.

archae-   ancient: e.g. archaeologist, archaic.

auto-   self: e.g. autobiography, automobile.

bene-   well: e.g. benefactor, benevolent.

bi, bis-   two, twice: e.g. bisect, bilingual, biennial.

cata, cath-   down, throughout: e.g. cataract, catapult, catholic.

circum-   round: e.g. circumference, circumnavigate, circumlocution.

cis-   on this side: e.g. cis-alphine.

con, (co, com, col, cor)-   with, together: e.g. connect, co-operate, combine, collaborate, corroborate.

contra, counter-   against: e.g. contradict, contravene, counteract, controvert.

de-   down, away from: e.g. descend, dethrone, degenerate, deflect, detract.

deca-   ten: e.g. decade, decagon, decalogue.

demi-   half: e.g. demi-god.

dia-   through: e.g. diameter, diagonal.

dis, dia-   in two: e.g. dissyllable.

dis, (di, diff)-   apart, asunder: e.g. differ, dispel, divert.

dys-   ill: e.g. dysentery.

epi-   upon: e.g. epitaph.

equi-   equal: e.g. equidistant, equivalent, equilibrium.

eu-   well: e.g. eulogy, euphony.

ex, ec-   out of, from: e.g. exodus, exhume, exclude, excavate, eccentric.

ex-   former: e.g. ex-policeman, ex-soldier, ex-convict.

extra-   beyond: e.g. extraordinary.

fore-   before: e.g. foretell, forefinger, forehead.

hemi-   half: e.g. hemisphere.

hepta-   seven: e.g. heptagon, heptarchy.

hetero-   different: e.g. heterogeneous, heterodox.

hexa-   six: e.g. hexagon, hexameter.

homo-   the same: e.g. homogeneous, homonym.

hyper-   beyond, above: e.g. hyperbole, hyper-sensitive.

hypo-   under: e.g. hypothesis.

in (ig, il, im, ir)-   not: (*These are used before adjectives*) e.g. invisible, ignoble, illegal, impure, irregular.

in (il, im, ir, em, en)-   into: (*These are used before verbs*) e.g. inject, illustrate, import, irrigate, encourage, embrace.

inter-   between: e.g. intervene, intermediate, intercept.

intro-   within: e.g. introduce.

juxta-   near to: e.g. juxtaposition.

mal, male-   bad: e.g. malefactor, malediction, malice, malcontent.

meta-   change: e.g. metaphor, metamorphosis, metonymy.

mis-   wrong: e.g. mislead, miscount.

mono-   alone, one: e.g. monarch, monoplane, monologue.

ne, non-   not: e.g. nonsense, negation.

ob (o, oc, of, op)-   against, in the way of: e.g. obstacle, obnoxious, omit, occasion, offend, oppose.

omni-   all, universal: e.g. omnipotent, omniscience, omnivorous.

para, par-   beside: e.g. parallel, parable.

pene-   almost: e.g. peninsula.

penta-   five: e.g. pentagon.

per-   through, thoroughly: e.g. perfect, percolate.

peri-   around: e.g. perimeter.

poly-   many: e.g. polygamist, polygon, polysyllabic.

post-   after: e.g. posthumous, post-mortem, postscript.

pre-   before: e.g. predecessor, preamble, precede.

preter- beyond: e.g. preternatural.

pro- for: e.g. pronoun, produce, propel.

pro- before: e.g. prologue, prognosticate.

pseudo- sham: e.g. pseudonym.

re- back, again: e.g. rediscover, react, rejoin, remit.

retro- backwards: e.g. retrograde, retrospect.

se- aside, apart: e.g. seclude, seduce, separate.

semi- half: e.g. semicircle, semicolon.

sine- without: e.g. sinecure.

sub- under: e.g. submarine, subordinate, subterranean.

super- above: e.g. superhuman, supernatural, superman, superfine.

sur- above: e.g. surmount.

trans- across: e.g. transport, transmit, transatlantic.

tri- three: e.g. triangle, tripod, triple, tricycle.

ultra- beyond: e.g. ultra-modern, ultra-violet, ultra-mundane.

vice- in place of, for: e.g. viceroy, vice-captain, vice-president.

SOME GEOGRAPHICAL FACTS
WORTH REMEMBERING

The earth: The earth on which we live is shaped like a ball; yet it is not quite round, being a little flattened at the poles and bulging slightly at the equator.

The axis of the earth is an imaginary line passing through its centre from pole to pole.

There are two poles—the North Pole and the South Pole.

The equator is an imaginary line drawn round the earth, midway between the two poles.

The circumference of the earth is approximately 39 900 km (24 800 miles). The diameter of the earth is roughly 12 900 km (8 000 miles).

The solar system: The sun is fixed, and moving around the sun are a number of large spheres called planets. The earth on which we live is one of those planets. Our moon is also a planet. Some of the other planets are Mercury, Venus, Mars, Jupiter, Saturn, Uranus and Neptune. The sun and all the planets around it are called the solar system.

The sun is 150 million km (93 million miles) away from the earth.

The moon is about 386 000 km (240 000 miles) away from the earth.

Motions of the earth: The earth has two motions: (a) diurnal or daily, and (b) annual or yearly.

Diurnal or daily motions: The earth rotates or turns on its axis from west to east once in twenty-four hours. This is called the rotation of the earth.

Rotation of the earth causes day and night. When that side of the earth on which we live is turned towards the sun, we have day; but when it is turned away from the sun we have night.

The annual or yearly motion: The earth turns not only on its axis. It also moves around the sun along an almost circular path called its

118

Orbit. This journey of the earth around the sun is called the revolution of the earth and it takes $365\frac{1}{4}$ days. Leaving out the $\frac{1}{4}$ day our ordinary year consists of 365 days; but at the end of every four years the four quarter-days are added to the ordinary year to make a **leap year** of 366 days.

Seasons: The axis of the earth is inclined at an angle of $66\frac{1}{2}°$ to the plane of its orbit. As a result of this the earth is in different positions as it makes its journey round the sun. The annual motion of the earth, on its inclined axis, therefore causes the four seasons of Spring, Summer, Autumn and Winter.

On 21 March the sun is overhead at the equator. It is then Spring in the North Temperate zone.

On 21 June when the sun is overhead at the Tropic of Cancer, places in the North Temperate zone have Summer.

On 23 September the sun is back on the Equator and the North Temperate zone has the season of Autumn.

On 21 December the sun is at the Tropic of Capricorn. Then the North Temperate zone has Winter.

In the South Temperate Zone the seasons are the reverse of those mentioned above at the same time of the year.

Equinoxes or equal nights (and consequently equal days) are the times when the sun is shining directly overhead at the Equator. 21 March is called the Vernal Equinox; 23 September is called the Autumnal Equinox.

Solstices are the times when the sun is overhead at the Tropics of Cancer and Capricorn and seems to stand for a little while before moving back in the direction of the Equator. 21 June is called the Summer Solstice, 21 December is called the Winter Solstice.

Distance: In order to enable us to calculate the distance between one place and another a number of circles are drawn round the globe. Every circle is divided into 360 degrees ($360°$) and each degree is approximately 112 km ($69\frac{1}{2}$ miles).

Lines of latitude and longitude enable us to measure distances on a map, or to find the position of any place on a map.

Latitude is distance, measured in degrees, north or south of the Equator.

Longitude is distance, measured in degrees, east or west of a given meridian.

Meridians or mid-day lines are lines drawn on a map from the North Pole to the South Pole, and all places on any one of these lines have mid-day at the same time.

The Prime Meridian passes through Greenwich. East longitude is up to 180° east of Greenwich. West longitude is up to 180° west of Greenwich.

THE FIVE CHIEF PARALLELS OF LATITUDE ARE:

The Equator marked 0°.
The Tropic of Cancer $23\frac{1}{2}$° north of the Equator.
The Tropic of Capricorn $23\frac{1}{2}$° south of the Equator.
The Arctic Circle $66\frac{1}{2}$° north of the Equator.
The Antarctic $66\frac{1}{2}$° south of the Equator.

TEMPERATURE BELTS OR ZONES

The above-named parallels of latitude divide the earth into five belts or zones corresponding to different kinds of climate.

(a) The North Frigid Zone from the Arctic Circle to the North Pole.

(b) The North Temperate Zone between the Tropic of Cancer and the Arctic Circle.

(c) The Torrid Zone on both sides of the Equator between the Tropic of Cancer and the Tropic of Capricorn.

(d) The South Temperate Zone between the Tropic of Capricorn and the Antarctic Circle.

(e) The South Frigid Zone between the Antarctic Circle and the South Pole.

The frigid zones have the coldest climate.
The torrid zone has the hottest climate.
The temperate zones are neither too hot nor too cold.

Time: Parallels of Longitude determine time. The time of a place depends on its longitude east or west of Greenwich. As the earth rotates from west to east, places to the east of Greenwich will come directly under the sun before those places to the west of Greenwich. Now the earth rotates through 360° in twenty-four hours, or 15° in 1 hour, or 1° in four minutes. Calcutta is approximately 90° east of Greenwich so that Calcutta will be $\frac{(90° \times 4)}{60}$ = 6 hours in advance of the time in London.

That is to say when it is noon in London it will be 6 p.m. in Calcutta.

Standard Time: As local time is found to vary constantly as one travels some distance from one place to another, there is usually an arrangement by which all places in a certain region or "belt" agree to use the same time. This is called Standard Time.

International Date Line: Meridian 180°E and Meridian 180°W are one and the same line, situated in the Pacific Ocean, near Fiji, Samoa, and Gilbert Islands. In reckoning time from Greenwich to this meridian, it is found that there is a difference of one day between Greenwich to 180°E and Greenwich to 180°W. In order to avoid confusion the International Date Line was agreed upon. Travellers crossing the meridian of 180° from the east add a day, while those from the west subtract a day, from the calendar.

Climate: The climate of a place is its average weather conditions calculated over a long period of time. Climate chiefly depends upon (a) temperature, (b) rainfall.

PRINCIPAL CLIMATES OF THE WORLD

TYPE OF CLIMATE	CHARACTERISTICS	TYPICAL AREAS
A. Hot Climates: 1. Equatorial.	Always very hot with a temperature of about 27°C. Little range of temperature—about 1–2 degrees. Rainfall throughout the year, 2000–2500 mm. Convectional rains. Evergreen forests.	Found stretching in a belt about 5 degrees on either side of the equator. The Congo Basin; Amazon Basin; The East Indies.
2. Savanna or Tropical grasslands.	Hot throughout the year. Rain during the hottest season. A long dry season.	Found to the north and south of the equatorial belt. The Sudan; Venezuela; Mexico; The Orinoco Basin.
3. Monsoon.	Always hot. Heavy rains during the hottest season.	India; Southern China; North Australia.

Principal Climates of the World (*contd.*)

TYPE OF CLIMATE	CHARACTERISTICS	TYPICAL AREAS
4. Hot Desert.	Always very hot and dry. Very little rainfall—less than 250 mm. Great range of temperature between days and nights— the days are hot, the nights cold.	The desert regions lie on the west of the continents along the Tropics of Cancer and Capricorn in the rain shadow areas, or in the centre of huge land masses. Sahara in Africa; Kalahari in S. Africa; Atacama in S. America; Desert of Arabia; Thar or Indian Desert; Australian Desert.
B. Temperate Climates: 5. Mediterranean.	Hot, dry summers; mild, cool, wet winters.	On the west side of the continents between Lat. 28–40 degrees. The whole region around the Mediterranean Sea; California; Central Chile; S.W. Australia; Southern part of the West Coast of South Africa.
6. Trade Wind, or Warm Temperate East Coast.	Hot, wet summers; cool, dry winters. Rain at all seasons.	Southern Brazil; S.E. United States, Central and N. China; Natal; Queensland in Australia.
7. Maritime, or Cool Temperate West Coast.	Warm summers; mild, cool winters. Small range of temperature. Rain throughout the year.	British Isles; West Europe; Br. Columbia; Southern Chile; New Zealand; Tasmania.
8. Continental.	Very hot summers; very cold winters. Considerable range of temperature. Rainfall chiefly in summer.	Central Canada; Mid-west U.S.A.; Southern Russia; South Siberia.
9. Temperate Desert.	Dry all through the year. Hot summers, cold winters.	Gobi in Central Asia. Desert of Iran or Persia.
C. Cold Climates: 10. Arctic, or Cold Desert.	Very long bitterly cold winters; very short, cold summers. Very little rainfall.	Lapland; N. Siberia; N. Canada. These regions are in the frigid zones.
11. Alpine, or Mountain.	Perpetual snow on the tops of the mountains.	The Alps in Italy and Switzerland; The Rockies in N. America; The Andes in S. America; The Himalayas in India.

A Natural Region is a part of the earth's surface having certain definite characteristics of climate and of plant and animal life.

Temperature is the degree of heat or cold in the atmosphere as measured by the thermometer. The temperature of a place is determined by (a) latitude, (b) altitude, or height above sea-level, (c) distance from the sea, (d) direction of the prevailing winds, (e) the presence of a cold or warm current, (f) slope of the land.

Wind: Wind is air in motion. The chief cause of winds is the difference in the pressure of the air. Heated air near the earth's surface, being light, rises into the higher regions while cold air from the surrounding regions move into this low pressure area to equalise the pressure of the atmosphere. This movement of the air is known as wind.

Winds blow from areas of high pressure to areas of low pressure.

Winds are named by the direction from which they blow, but the deflection of the winds is due to the rotation of the earth. Winds are deflected to the right in the Northern Hemisphere, and to the left in the Southern Hemisphere.

Winds are divided into three main groups:
1. Regular—e.g. trade winds, westerlies.
2. Periodical—blowing at certain seasons—e.g. monsoons.
3. Variables—e.g. cyclones and other local winds.

Trade Winds: The steady currents of air blowing towards the equator from the north-east and the south-east are known as the Trade Winds. They are so called because they were of great use to sailing ships, which did the carrying trade of the world before the invention of steamships.

Monsoons are seasonal winds which blow briefly over India, Indo-China, China and North-west Australia. In summer, due chiefly to the high temperature over the land masses, the pressure is low, and thus the winds blow from the sea to the land bringing a great deal of rain. In winter the reverse is the case. A monsoon climate, therefore enjoys summer rains and winter drought.

The Westerlies are regular winds which blow outside of the tropics in the Temperate Zones. The south-westerly winds blow in the Northern Hemisphere and the north-westerly winds in the Southern Hemisphere.

South of Latitude 40° the absence of land masses enables these winds to gather great force and thus they are known as **Roaring Forties.**

Chinook are hot, dry winds on the east or leeward side of the Rocky Mountains (Rain Shadow area). As these winds descend from the mountains they are pressed down and become heated. Similar winds on the north of the Alps are called Föhn.

The Sirocco is a hot, moist wind which blows from the Sahara desert across to Italy.

The Solano is a similar wind blowing from the Sahara to the Iberian Peninsula.

The Harmattan is a hot dry wind blowing from the interior of West Africa.

The Mistral is a very cold wind which blows down from the plateau of Central France.

The Bora is a cold, dry wind blowing outwards from Hungary to the north of Italy.

Punas are cold dry winds blowing down on the western side of the Andes.

Cyclones are irregular local winds which swirl round and round a low pressure area. They are chiefly found in latitudes 35° to 60°.

Anticyclones are similar winds swirling round a high pressure centre.

Hurricane: A hurricane is a severe tropical storm which revolves around a centre of low pressure. It travels at a terrific speed, usually between 160 and 240 km per hour. In approaching the centre it moves in an anti-clockwise direction, and in departing it moves in the opposite direction. In the middle of a hurricane there is usually a lull or calm. The lull occurs when the hurricane has spent about half its force. Then the winds begin to blow in the opposite direction, and the hurricane rages as violently as before for the other half of its life.

A hurricane does considerable damage to life and property. There are many islands in the West Indies which lie in the path of hurricanes. Fortunately, certain warning signs give notice of its approach. There is a rise in the barometer, a fall in the thermometer, and a disappearance of land and sea breezes.

Blizzard is a blinding storm of snow and wind common in the polar regions.

Typhoon is the name given to a cyclone which occurs over the China seas.

Tornadoes are violent cyclonic storms which occcur in some parts of the United States and cause great destruction.

Ocean Currents are streams of water crossing the oceans. They follow the direction of the prevailing winds.

Beginning in the Atlantic Ocean, the westerly winds drive the cold **Antarctic Current** eastwards. This turns northwards when it reaches the coast of Africa and is known as the **Benguela Current**. The South East Trade Winds take this current westwards as the **South Equatorial Current.** Off Cape St Roque at the corner of Brazil this current divides into two. One branch flows south-west to become the **Brazilian Current** while the main current continues north-west into the Gulf of Mexico. This South Equatorial Current leaves the Gulf of Mexico and flows north-east as the **Warm Gulf Stream**. It widens over the Atlantic, part flowing as the **North Atlantic Drift** and warming the shores of the British Isles and Northern Europe. The other part turns south at the Canaries under the influence of the North East Trade Winds to join the **North Equatorial Current**. From the Arctic Ocean come the cold **Arctic Current** flowing along the shores of Greenland, and the cold **Labrador Current.** The latter meets the warm Gulf Stream off Newfoundland. The meeting of the cold air and warm air from over these two currents causes great fogs off Newfoundland. (Trace these currents on a map of the world showing currents.)

In the Pacific Ocean the currents are similar to those in the Atlantic but the names are different. The Antarctic Current joins the **Peruvian Current** which is continued as the South Equatorial Current. Off the East of Australia this current divides into the **New South Wales Current** which turns south, while the main current continues to become **Japan** or **Kuro Siwo Current**—the counterpart of the Gulf Stream. When this current turns southwards it becomes the **Californian Current**.

The currents of the north Indian Ocean follow the monsoons. Those of the South Indian Ocean follow the pattern of the Atlantic and Pacific. The most important current in this part of the ocean is the **Agulhas Current**.

Ocean Currents influence climate. Places near to a warm current have a much warmer climate than lands in the same latitude under the influence of a cold current.

Rain: By a process called EVAPORATION the heat of the sun changes much of the water of seas, rivers and lakes into water-vapour.

When this moisture-laden air ascends into the colder higher regions of the atmosphere or is blown there by winds, it becomes cooled, and condensation takes place. The drops of water then unite and fall to the earth as rain.

The chief types of rainfall are convectional, relief, cyclonic.

Dew: During the night the earth cools more rapidly than the air above it. The layers of air nearest the earth therefore become cooled. Condensation takes place and the moisture deposited on the ground, grass and other objects is called dew.

Rainbow: The sun's rays passing through the drops of water in the air are doubly refracted and the human eye sees the reflection in the form of a brilliant arch of prismatic colours which we call the rainbow. A rainbow is best seen when the rain is falling while the sun is shining.

Clouds are collections of water-vapour on the dust particles in the various layers of the atmosphere. They are usually classified as follows: cirrus (feathery); cumulus (rounded masses); stratus (horizontal sheets); nimbus (rain).

Fogs and Mist are formed when condensation of the water-vapour in the air near the earth's surface takes place upon the dust particles in the air.

"A fog is a cloud resting on the earth; a cloud is a fog floating high in the air." (Huxley.)

Snow: If the temperature in the upper layers of the atmosphere falls below freezing-point then the moisture in the air is frozen into little six-sided crystals. These crystals fall to the earth as snow, but only when the temperature over the earth's surface is also near to freezing-point.

Snow Line: The level above which there is always snow.

Hail is caused by the freezing of raindrops as they pass through layers of cold air. Hence hail falls to the ground in showers of little hard pellets.

Eclipse: When the light of the sun or the moon is obscured by another body passing between it and the eye, the sun or moon is said to be in eclipse.

The sun is in eclipse when the moon comes between it and the earth.

There is an eclipse of the moon when the earth comes between it and the sun.

Land and Sea Breezes: Land heats more rapidly and cools more quickly than the sea.

During the day, therefore, the pressure of the air over the land is lower than that over the sea. Hence breezes blow from the sea to the land.

At night the air over the sea is warmer than the air over the land so that the breeze blows from the land to the sea.

Tides: These are the regular rise and fall of the waters of the ocean. Tides are caused by the attractive force of the sun and moon acting upon the earth and on the moving waters of the ocean. There are two kinds of tides. (a) Spring tides, which are caused by the pulling of the sun and moon together; and (b) Neap tides, which are caused when the sun and moon are at right-angles and pull against each other. There are two Spring tides and two Neap tides every lunar month.

Spring tide is when the highest point of the tide is reached. Neap tide is when the lowest point of the tide is reached.

The flow of the tide is the coming in.

The ebb of the tide is the going out.

Tides ebb and flow twice in 24 hours.

Work of the Tides: Tides alter the shape of the coast line. They form estuaries when they rush up the mouth of a narrow river.

They sometimes form bores, as in the Severn; and capes, as when they bring material and deposit it on the continental shelf e.g. The Cape of Good Hope.

They aid shipping.

Saltiness of the sea: The water of rivers absorbs tiny particles of mineral salts from the earth which eventually reach the sea. In the course of centuries these accumulated deposits have made the sea water salt.

Continental shelf is the name given to the land around the continents which is covered by the sea. The shelf slopes down to a depth of 100 fathoms (183 metres), from which edge there is a steep drop to the bed of the ocean. Continental shelves provide excellent fishing grounds and good harbours.

The earth's crust is composed of rocks which are classified as either (a) igneous, (b) aqueous or sedimentary or stratified, (c) metamorphic.

Volcanoes: A volcano is an opening in the earth's crust out of which steam, gases and molten rocks are hurled with terrific force.

The interior of the earth is very hot. Through cracks in the earth's surface water from the rain, rivers, seas etc., trickles down to the interior of the earth where it boils and is changed into steam. This is kept down by the pressure of the layers of the earth. At certain times the steam forces itself through a fault or a line of weakness in the earth. When this happens an eruption of a volcano is said to have taken place.

Volcanoes may be either active, dormant or extinct.

Geysers are hot springs from which columns of boiling water and steam gush forth at intervals. Geysers are found in regions usually associated with volcanoes. Iceland; The Yellowstone Park in Wyoming, North America; and New Zealand are famous for geysers.

An earthquake is the shaking or movement of the earth. As the interior of the earth cools it solidifies and leaves spaces between the layers of the earth. The crusts of the earth then fall or move to fit themselves on the shrinking interior. When this happens we feel the movements as earthquakes.

Fold mountains are caused by earthquakes and are found along the lines of weakness of the earth.

Block mountains are solid masses of hard resistant rocks which have been able to withstand the movements which cause folding of the earth's surface.

Valleys: When forces working inside the earth cause a block mountain to split, the "rift" thus made is known as a **Rift Valley**.
  When a valley runs parallel to the trend of the mountains it is **Longitudinal**; when it runs across it is **Transverse.**

A canyon is a steep-side gully carved out by a river flowing through a rainless region.

Isobars are lines which are drawn on a map to connect places of equal pressure.

Isotherms are lines drawn on a map to connect places having equal temperature.

Isohyets are lines drawn on a map to connect places of equal rainfall.

Contours are lines drawn on a map to connect places of equal height above sea level.

Shotts is the name of the plateau in North-West Africa between the Atlas Mountains and the Tell.

A shott is a shallow lake which becomes dry in the hot season.

Tell: The Tell is the most important region of the Republic of Algeria in North-West Africa. It is a fertile coastal strip between the Algerian Plateau and the sea.

Veld: The Veld or High Veld is a rich grassland country in the eastern part of the plateau of South Africa. Most of the Transvaal, the Orange Free State and part of Cape Colony belong to it. Large flocks of sheep are reared on the Veld chiefly for wool.

Steppes are the great temperate grasslands of Southern Russia.
Karroos: The Karroo is a natural region of South Africa between the

coastlands and the Plateau. There are two Karroos, the Little Karroo and the Great Karroo. The vegetation in the Karroos is poor and the main industries are sheep farming and ostrich rearing.

Karst is a barren region on the coast of the Adriatic Sea.

Landes are an area of sand dunes on the south coast of France near Bordeaux.

Polders are the areas of land in Holland below sea level which are enclosed by the embankments and dykes. Machinery for pumping water is a feature of the polders.

Cantons: The term used to describe the political divisions of Switzerland.

Water table: The margin of the earth below which the layers of soil are saturated with water.

A tributary is the name given to a stream which empties itself into the main river as it flows to the sea. A tributary is also known as an affluent.

A confluence is the place where a tributary joins the main stream.

A flood plain is a plain which is liable to flooding by the overflowing of a river which has become swollen by heavy rains or melting snows. A flood plain is built up of deposits of fertile alluvial soil left by the river after the floods have subsided.

A waterfall is a steep descent or fall in the flowing of a river. Large waterfalls are called cataracts; smaller ones are known as cascades.

An avalanche is a mass of snow and ice which breaks loose from the snow-clad mountains and slips down the mountain sides with terrific force.

A glacier is a huge sheet of ice formed from compressed snow which glides slowly down the mountain sides or valleys.

A moraine is the name given to the debris after a glacier has melted.

An iceberg is the name given to a large mass of ice floating in the sea Icebergs are really parts of a glacier which break off and fall into the sea when the glacier reaches the coast unmelted. The bulk of an iceberg is submerged, only about one-tenth being visible above the surface of the water.

The largest ocean in the world	Pacific Ocean, about $166\,000\,000\,km^2$ in area
The longest rivers in the world	Mississippi, 7244 km
	Amazon, 6436 km
	Nile, 6670 km
	Yangste, 5471 km
The shallowest sea in the world	Baltic Sea
The greatest ocean depth	Challenger Deep 11 035 metres (off Guam-Pacific)
The largest island in the world	Greenland
The largest lake in the world (excluding Caspian Sea)	Lake Superior in N.A., 616 km long
The largest lake in North America	Lake Superior
The largest lake in South America	Lake Titicaca, in Bolivia
The largest body of fresh water in Asia	Lake Baikal
The largest river in Europe	Volga
The longest canal in the world	The Grand Canal of China
The greatest seaport in the world	Rotterdam
The greatest meat-producing country in the world	Argentina, S.A.
The highest chain of mountains in the world	Himalayas
The highest chain of mountains in Europe	Alps
The highest peak in the world	Mt. Everest, 8840 m
The highest peak in the Andes	Aconcagua, Chile, 6968 m
The highest mountain in Europe	Mt. Blanc, 4877 m
The most mountainous country in Europe	Switzerland
The highest active volcano in the world	Cotopaxi, Ecuador, 5968 m
The hottest region in the world	Sahara Desert
The coldest inhabited place in the world	Verkhoyansk
The longest day (in the Northern Hemisphere)	21 June
The shortest day (in the Northern Hemisphere)	21 December
The longest day (in the Southern Hemisphere)	21 December
The shortest day (in the Southern Hemisphere)	21 June
The greatest centre of the silk industry	Lyons, in France
A country in Europe famous for its cart-horses	Belgium
The land of windmills	Holland

The greatest oil-producing countries in the Commonwealth
Nigeria, Britain and Canada
The highest waterfall in the world Angel Falls, Venezuela, 1005 m
The largest equatorial forest in the world The Amazon Basin

COMMODITIES AND FIVE LARGEST SUPPLIERS (in order)

COMMODITY	CHIEF SOURCES OF SUPPLY
Wheat	Soviet Union, United States, China, India, France
Maize	United States, China, Brazil, Rumania, France
Rice	China, India, Indonesia, Bangladesh, Thailand
Cocoa	Ivory Coast, Brazil, Ghana, Nigeria, Cameroon
Coffee	Brazil, Colombia, Ivory Coast, Indonesia, Mexico
Tea	India, China, Sri Lanka, Turkey, Japan
Sugar	Cuba, Soviet Union, Brazil, India, United States
Cotton	United States, Soviet Union, China, India, Pakistan
Wool	Australia, Soviet Union, New Zealand, Argentina, South Africa
Jute	India, China, Bangladesh, Thailand, Burma
Barley	Soviet Union, China, France, United Kingdom, Canada
Oats	Soviet Union, United States, West Germany, Canada, Poland
Tobacco	China, United States, India, Brazil, Turkey
Grapes	Italy, France, Spain, Soviet Union, United States
Nickel Ore	Soviet Union, Canada, New Caledonia, Australia, Cuba
Diamonds	Zaire, Soviet Union, South Africa, Botswana, Ghana
Rubber	Malaysia, Indonesia, Thailand, Sri Lanka, India
Gold	South Africa, Soviet Union, Canada, United States, Papua New Guinea
Silver	Mexico, Soviet Union, Peru, Canada, United States
Tin	Malaysia, Thailand, Bolivia, Indonesia, China
Copper	United States, Soviet Union, Japan, Chile, Zambia
Petroleum	United States, Japan, France, Italy, West Germany
Iron	Soviet Union, Australia, United States, China, Brazil
Coal	United States, China, Soviet Union, Poland, United Kingdom

COMMODITIES AND FIVE LARGEST SUPPLIERS (in order)
(*contd.*)

COMMODITY	CHIEF SOURCES OF SUPPLY
Salt	United States, China, Soviet Union, West Germany, United Kingdom
Zinc Ore	Canada, Soviet Union, Australia, Peru, United States
Lead Ore	Soviet Union, United States, Australia, Canada, China

COUNTRIES OF AFRICA

COUNTRIES	CAPITAL	AREA (sq. km)	POP. (millions)
Algeria	Algiers	295,033	18.2
Angola	Luanda	1,246,700	5.8
Benin	Porto Novo	112,600	3.2
Burkina	Ouagadougou	274,200	7.1
Botswana	Gaborone	575,000	0.8
Burundi	Bujumbura	27,834	4.4
Cameroon	Yaounde	474,000	8.5
Central African Empire	Bangui	617,000	2.4
Chad	N'Djamene	1,284,000	4.6
Comoro Islands	Moroni	2,170	0.3
Congo	Brazzaville	331,850	1.6
Djibouti	Djibouti	23,000	0.1
Egypt	Cairo	1,000,000	36.4
Equatorial Guinea	Malabo	28,051	0.3
Ethiopia	Addis Ababa	1,000,000	30.4
Gabon	Libreville	267,000	0.6
Gambia	Banjul	9,300	0.6
Ghana	Accra	238,537	11.3
Guinea	Conakry	245,857	5.1
Guinea-Bissau	Bissau	36,125	0.8
Ivory Coast	Abidjan	322,463	8.6

Countries of Africa (*contd.*)

COUNTRIES	CAPITAL	AREA (sq. km)	POP. (millions)
Kenya	Nairobi	582,600	15.8
Lesotho	Maseru	30,340	1.3
Liberia	Monrovia	111,000	1.8
Libya	Tripoli	1,759,540	3.1
Madagascar	Tananarive	587,041	7.6
Malawi	Lilongwe	118,000	5.9
Mali	Bamako	1,204,021	6.8
Mauritania	Nouakchott	1,070,700	1.7
Mauritius	Port Louis	1,865	0.9
Morocco	Rabat	540,000	19.5
Mozambique	Maputo	784,961	12.7
Namibia	Windhoek	823,145	1.0
Niger	Niamey	1,187,000	5.1
Nigeria	Lagos	923,773	95.0
Rep. of South Africa	Cape Town and Pretoria	1,221,042	23.9
Réunion	Saint-Denis	2,510	0.5
Rwanda	Kigali	26,330	5.1
Senegal	Dakar	197,161	5.7
Seychelles	Victoria	375	0.6
Sierra Leone	Freetown	73,326	3.4
Somali Republic	Mogadishu	700,000	3.6
Sudan	Khartoum	2,500,000	18.4
Swaziland	Mbabane	17,400	0.6
Tanzania	Dar es Salaam	939,936	17.6
Togo	Lomé	56,000	2.8
Tunisia	Tunis	164,150	6.4
Uganda	Kampala	236,037	13.2
Western Sahara	El Aainn	266,000	0.08
Zaire	Kinshasa	2,345,409	28.3
Zambia	Lusaka	752,262	6
Zimbabwe	Harare	390,622	7.5

REVISION NOTES IN ENGLISH

GENDER

Gender is an easy subject, well treated in most grammar books. The student should especially note the following:

The feminine gender is denoted in three ways

(i) By a suffix, *e.g.* actor—actress.

(ii) By a word prefixed to another word, *e.g.* cock-sparrow; hen-sparrow.

(iii) By an entirely different word, *e.g.* drake—duck.

Masculine	Feminine	Masculine	Feminine
author	authoress	gaffer	gammer
bachelor	maid, spinster	gander	goose
baron	baroness	gentleman	lady
beau	belle	hart	roe
billy-goat	nanny-goat	he	she
boar	sow	heir	heiress
bridegroom	bride	hero	heroine
buck	doe	him	her
buck-rabbit	doe-rabbit	horse	mare
bull	cow	instructor	instructress
bullock	heifer	jack-ass	jenny-ass
cob	pen	lad	lass
colt	filly	lord	lady
count	countess	margrave	margravine
czar	czarina	marquis	marchioness
don	donna	mayor	mayoress
drone	bee	milter	spawner
duke	duchess	monk	nun
earl	countess	nephew	niece
emperor	empress	ram	ewe
executor	executrix	signor	signora
fox	vixen	sir	madam
friar	nun	sire	dam

Masculine	Feminine	Masculine	Feminine
sloven	slut, slattern	tutor	governess
spinner	spinster	uncle	aunt
stallion	mare	viceroy	vicereine
steer	heifer	viscount	viscountess
sultan	sultana	votary	votress
swain	nymph	wether	ewe
tom-cat	tabby-cat	widower	widow
traitor	traitress	wizard	witch
tsar	tsarina	waiter	waitress

THE POSSESSIVE CASE

The possessive (or genitive) is the case which denotes the owner or possessor, *e.g.* uncle's bicycle; ladies' hats; children's toys.

The possessive case is very important. Study the following rules.

Rules for forming the Possessive Case

1. The possessive case of nouns is formed by adding 's (apostrophe s) to the singular: *e.g.* The boy's ball; the child's toys; the man's hat.

2. If the plural ends in s the apostrophe only is added, *e.g.* The boys' ball.

3. If the plural does not end in s then the apostrophe s ('s) must be added: *e.g.* The children's toys; The men's hats.

4. With abstract nouns ending in *ss* or *ce* the apostrophe only is added. These are usually found in such phrases as: for goodness' sake; for righteousness' sake; for conscience' sake.

5. The sign of the possessive is put on the last word of:
   (a) Compound nouns: *e.g.* He lives at his father-in-law's house.
   (b) Nouns followed by a qualifying phrase: *e.g.* The winner of the race's prize.

6. As regards names note the following: We say Jones's birthday but the Joneses' residence.

FORMATION OF NOUNS, ADJECTIVES, VERBS AND ADVERBS

Below is set out a number of these words with the answers supplied in every case. To facilitate revision they are arranged in groups of ten. You should add to this list any other words you come across.

Word	Noun Formed	Word	Noun Formed
ferocious	ferocity	just	justice
sit	seat	injure	injury
compare	comparison	thumb	thimble
weigh	weight	high	height
penitent	penitence	laugh	laughter
abundant	abundance	poet	poetry
noble	nobility	false	falsehood
honest	honesty	solitary	solitude
grand	grandeur	die	death
serve	service	join	joint
fail	failure	decide	decision
fix	fixture	think	thought
mix	mixture	know	knowledge
scarce	scarcity	gird	girth
coal	colliery	defend	defence
wise	wisdom	slow	slowness, sloth
king	kingdom	grow	growth
prosper	prosperity	warm	warmth
shady	shade	slave	slavery
perform	performance	conquer	conquest
dry	dryness	lose	loss
wed	wedlock, wedding	proud	pride
child	childhood	decide	decision
free	freedom	humble	humility
broad	breadth	heroic	heroism
vale	valley	clean	cleanliness
neighbour	neighbourhood	long	length
hill	hillock	fly	flight
true	truth	strong	strength
save	saviour	destroy	destruction

Word	Noun Formed
friend	friendship
kind	kindness
bond	bondage
prove	proof
wide	width
draw	draught
lenient	lenience, leniency
judge	judgment
please	pleasure
merry	merriment
curious	curiosity
deep	depth
sell	sale
angry	anger
exhaust	exhaustion
pursue	pursuit
bag	baggage
fragrant	fragrance
anxious	anxiety
punctual	punctuality
regular	regularity
depart	departure
applaud	applause
loyal	loyalty
young	youth
behave	behaviour
discreet	discretion
pure	purity
enter	entrance
bury	burial
vain	vanity
busy	business
cruel	cruelty
able	ability
invade	invasion
reveal	revelation
holy	holiness
explain	explanation
extend	extension
accommodate	accommodation

Word	Noun Formed
innocent	innocence
hinder	hindrance
timid	timidity
absurd	absurdity
intimate	intimacy
excellent	excellence
submit	submission
analyse	analysis
awful	awe
lend	loan
candid	candour
ardent	ardour
zealous	zeal
splendid	splendour
marry	marriage
provide	provision
gay	gaiety
seize	seizure

Word	Adjective Formed
flax	flaxen
favour	favourable
metal	metallic
fortune	fortunate
music	musical
honour	honourable
danger	dangerous
fury	furious
circle	circular
talk	talkative
wool	woollen
attract	attractive
sense	sensible
extend	extensive
disaster	disastrous
ash	ashen
asp	aspen
wood	wooden
wit	witty
skill	skilful

Word	Adjective Formed	Word	Adjective Formed
ocean	oceanic	vigour	vigorous
pity	pitiable	energy	energetic
prosper	prosperous	zeal	zealous
mercy	merciful	enthusiasm	enthusiastic
Italy	Italian	smoke	smoky
France	French	fish	fishy
Spain	Spanish	notice	noticeable
angel	angelic	machine	mechanical
study	studious	courage	courageous
poet	poetical	help	helpful
imagine	imaginary	victory	victorious
fool	foolish	man	manly
palace	palatial	woman	womanly
providence	providential	Cyprus	Cypriot
child	childish	fame	famous
continued	continual, continuous	athlete	athletic
winter	wintry	law	lawful
autumn	autumnal	caution	cautious
equator	equatorial	custom	customary
equinox	equinoctial	parish	parochial
joy	joyful, joyous	tide	tidal
rhyme	rhythmical	bible	biblical
charity	charitable	crime	criminal
people	popular, populous	grief	grievous
decide	decisive	tire	tiresome
force	forceful, forcible	mourn	mournful
defend	defensive	war	warlike
Turk	Turkish	occasion	occasional
mountain	mountainous	social	sociable
picture	picturesque	prime	primitive
sheep	sheepish	memory	memorial, memorable
spirit	spiritous	adventure	adventurous
mischief	mischievous	instant	instantaneous
quarrel	quarrelsome	comfort	comfortable
humour	humorous	life	lifelike, lively
accident	accidental	comic	comical
plenty	plentiful, plenteous	prophet	prophetic
Canada	Canadian	art	artful, artless
father	fatherly	nation	national
mother	motherly	magnet	magnetic

Word	Adjective Formed
describe	descriptive
glory	glorious
chaos	chaotic
abyss	abysmal
title	titular
benefit	beneficial
respect	respectable
valour	valiant
nature	natural
habit	habitual
courage	courageous
merit	meritorious
punish	punitive
governor	gubernatorial
office	official
essence	essential
sloth	slothful
luxury	luxurious
volcano	volcanic
choir	choral
parent	parental
Wales	Welsh
science	scientific
Alsace	Alsatian

Word	Verb Formed
courage	encourage
strong	strengthen
fast	fasten
breath	breathe
new	renew
electric	electrify
clean	cleanse
notice	notify
simple	simplify
peril	imperil
sweet	sweeten

Word	Verb Formed
thought	think
cloth	clothe
gold	gilded
circle	encircle
false	falsify
fruit	fructify
beauty	beautify
angry	anger
pure	purify
sight	see
hard	harden
clear	clarify
fine	refine
solid	solidify
resolution	resolve
humble	humiliate
solution	solve
vigour	invigorate
fertile	fertilise
black	blacken
brass	braze
low	lower
solemn	solemnise
knee	kneel
glory	glorify
light	lighten
danger	endanger
bright	brighten
belief	believe
stupid	stupefy
glass	glaze
slave	enslave
person	personify
liquid	liquefy
head	behead
power	empower
equal	equalise
broad	broaden
friend	befriend

Word	Verb Formed	Word	Verb Formed
suspicion	suspect	glad	gladden
large	enlarge	hot	heat
endurance	endure	fat	fatten
custom	accustom	tight	tighten
poor	impoverish	loose	loosen
freedom	free	safe	save
nation	nationalise	bath	bathe
success	succeed	trust	entrust
calm	becalm	deep	deepen
peace	pacify	wide	widen
high	heighten	long	lengthen
division	divide	less	lessen
company	accompany	food	feed
people	popularise	noble	ennoble
judgment	judge	cheap	cheapen
product	produce	mad	madden
siege	besiege	smooth	smoothen
pleasure	please	modern	modernise
strife	strive	unison	unite
memory	memorise	soft	soften
rich	enrich	terror	terrify
certain	certify	vacant	vacate
sympathy	sympathise	sale	sell
creation	create	joy	enjoy
tale	tell	slaughter	slay
camp	encamp	pursuit	pursue
able	enable	thought	think
song	sing	liberty	liberate
force	enforce	health	heal
loss	lose		

Word	Verb Formed
roll	enroll
dictation	dictate
speech	speak
deed	do
shelf	shelve
lively	enliven
drama	dramatise
comparison	compare
feeble	enfeeble
sad	sadden

Word	Adverb Formed
valour	valiantly
free	freely
annual	annually
menace	menacingly
history	historically
happy	happily
true	truly
noble	nobly

Word	Adverb Formed	Word	Adverb Formed
sincere	sincerely	sympathy	sympathetically
able	ably	note	notably
vain	vainly	natural	naturally
remark	remarkably	office	officially
occasion	occasionally	merit	meritoriously
whole	wholly	pleasant	pleasantly
necessary	necessarily	ideal	ideally
honour	honourably	will	wilfully
first	firstly	design	designedly
last	lastly	art	artfully
hope	hopefully	skill	skilfully

ANTONYMS

(Graded from simple to difficult, and arranged in groups of ten)

Word	Opposite	Word	Opposite
cold	hot	absent	present
dry	wet	poor	rich
love	hate, hatred	right	wrong
question	answer	win	lose
asleep	awake	peace	war
front	back	coarse	fine
joy	sorrow, grief	rough	smooth
begin	end, cease	top	bottom
find	lose	buy	sell
friend	enemy, foe	life	death
dead	alive	proud	humble
busy	idle	easy	difficult, hard
sweet	sour, acid, bitter	cheap	dear, expensive
bright	dull	inside	outside
rise	fall, sink	give	take
true	false	hit	miss
quick	slow	wide	narrow
start	finish	loud	soft
ugly	beautiful	clean	dirty
near	far, distant	weep	laugh

Antonyms (*contd.*)

Word	Opposite	Word	Opposite
kind	cruel	collect	disperse
empty	full	youth	age
ever	never	modern	ancient
bless	curse	former	latter
adult	child	least	greatest
north	south	slender	stout
east	west	robust	feeble, delicate
high	low	good	bad
upper	lower	big	small
higher	lower	smart, clever	foolish, stupid
better	worse	here	there
entrance	exit	first	last
active	passive	early	late
noise	silence	fat	thin, lean
quiet	noisy	join, unite	separate
inner	outer	light	heavy, darkness
lend	borrow	day	night
go	come	many	few
hard	soft	all	none
old	new	often	seldom
junior	senior	fresh	stale
live	die	straight	crooked
long	short	weak	strong
enjoy	dislike	deep	shallow
gay	grave	open	shut, closed
rejoice	mourn, grieve	black	white
pleasant	disagreeable	praise	blame
success	failure	this	that
harmony	discord	these	those
blessing	curse	morning	evening
generous	mean, selfish	summer	winter
valour	cowardice	young	old
bravery	cowardice	giant	dwarf
advance	retreat, retire	wild	tame
arrive	depart	profit, gain	loss
attack	defend	happy	sad
before	behind	daily	nightly
engage	dismiss	health	sickness, disease
appear	vanish	lead	follow
everywhere	nowhere	land	water

Antonyms (contd.)

Word	Opposite	Word	Opposite
earth	sea	bow	stern
hill	valley	stationary	moving
mountain	plain	dynamic	static
right	left	centrifugal	centripetal
public	private	oriental	occidental
acute	obtuse	miser	spendthrift
lazy	industrious	spacious	limited
master	servant	sober	intoxicated
arrive	depart	future	past
remember	forget	abundance	scarcity
appoint	dismiss	common	rare
knowledge	ignorance	simple	complex
pale	ruddy	barren	fruitful
raw	cooked	ally	enemy
help	hinder	flow	ebb
accept	reject, refuse	teach	learn
natural	artificial	think	guess
polite	saucy	work	rest
summit	base	worker	drone
apex	base	truth	error
cloudy	clear	familiar	strange
dawn	dusk	freedom	captivity
ascend	descend	poverty	riches
vacant	occupied	extravagance	thrift
hope	despair	danger	safety
interior	exterior	sacred	profane
permanent	temporary	virtue	vice
obey	command	wisdom	folly
negative	positive	within	without
conceal	reveal	polite	rude
hide	show	proper	common
singular	plural	saint	sinner
foreign	native	height	depth
smile	frown	asleep	awake
multiply	divide	convex	concave
wax	wane	agree	contradict
prosperity	adversity	bashful	bold
victory	defeat	indolent	diligent
superior	inferior	inhale	exhale
level	steep	expand	contract

Antonyms *(contd.)*

Word	Opposite	Word	Opposite
liquid	solid	victor	vanquished
pardon	punish	real	imaginary
complainant	defendant	antecedent	consequent
debtor	creditor	eager	reluctant
rural	urban	order	chaos
emigrant	immigrant	certain	doubt
optimist	pessimist	affirmative	negative
ingenuous	insincere	venial	unpardonable
numerous	sparse	liquid	solid
transparent	translucent, opaque	rigid	flexible
pedestrian	passenger	novice	veteran
powerful	feeble	industry	sloth
guilty	innocent	genuine	counterfeit
hell	Heaven	accelerate	retard
heroic	base	celestial	terrestrial
ancestor	progeny	benevolent	malevolent
assemble	disperse	benediction	malediction
condemn	exonerate	compulsory	voluntary
slim	chubby, stout	compulsory	optional
minimum	maximum	obligatory	voluntary
arrival	departure	analysis	synthesis
reward	punishment	excess	shortage
economy	extravagance	surplus	deficit
increase	decrease	prosperous	indigent
majority	minority	assent	dissent
employ	dismiss	consent	dissent
liberty	slavery	include	exclude
lawful	illegal	indigenous	exotic
transverse	longitudinal	apprehend	release
attract	distract	gaiety	melancholy
amateur	professional	solitary	populous
confine	release	sparse	populated
orthodox	heterodox	predecessor	successor
pure	adulterated	confusion	orderliness
lovely	repulsive	pleasure	pain
graceful	hideous	convict	acquit
pugnacious	peaceful	concurrent	consecutive
theory	practice	poison	antidote
hostile	friendly	prolific	sterile
Gentile	Jew	initial	final

Antonyms (contd.)

Word	Opposite	Word	Opposite
monotony	variety	regularly	periodically
survive	succumb	submissive	intractible
prospective	retrospective	incessantly	rarely
premature	overdue	monogamy	polygamy
caution	recklessness	prologue	epilogue
force, compel	persuade	latitude	longitude
colleague	antagonist	precept	example
prudence	indiscretion	ancestry	posterity
motionless	agitated	creditor	debtor
exact	inaccurate	prose	verse

The following pairs of words, although not true opposites, are often used as such, and may be grouped with these:

parent-child, nephew-uncle, aunt-niece, teacher-pupil, guardian-ward, master-servant, mistress-servant, employer-employee, clergy-laity, soul-body, king-subject, landlord-tenant, lawyer-client, doctor-patient, lecturer-student, host-guest, wholesale-retail, vowel-consonant, hunger-thirst, captain-crew, demand-supply, cause-effect, lender-borrower.

SYNONYMS

abandon .... desert, forsake, leave.
abbreviate ... curtail, abridge, compress.
abundant.... ample, copious, plentiful.
adore...... worship, idolise.
alive ...... lively, vivacious.
ally .... colleague, helper, partner, accomplice.
alms ...... offertory, dole, gratuity.
amend..... improve, ameliorate.
anxiety .... misgiving, foreboding, solicitude.
assent ...... consent, acquiesce, agree.

bad....... evil, wicked, devilish, naughty, worthless.
beautify..... adorn, decorate.
beg .... implore, solicit, supplicate, beseech.
behaviour ... conduct, demeanour, deportment.
big .... enormous, gigantic, huge, mighty, great, vast, immense, large, majestic, bulky.
biography ... memoir
blame ..... censure, upbraid, reprove.
blessing .... benediction, benison.

Synonyms (*contd.*)

brave . . . . courageous, fearless, daring, intrepid.

bright . . . . . . clear, brilliant, lustrous, transparent, intelligent.

brittle . . . . . . frail, fragile.

burglar . . . . . bandit, highwayman, thief, brigand.

busy . . . . industrious, diligent, active, assiduous, alert, nimble, lively, energetic.

candid . . . . . . frank, sincere, straightforward, outspoken, open, ingenuous.

care . . . . solicitude, anxiety.

catch . . . . capture, seize, arrest, apprehend.

cause . . . . reason, purpose, motive.

character . . . . reputation.

charity . . . . . . benevolence, philanthropy.

choose . . . . . . select, discriminate, differentiate.

clever . . . . . . ingenious, versatile, precocious.

clothes . . . . . . attire, dress, garb, apparel, raiment.

confess . . . . . admit, apologise, own, acknowledge.

constant . . . . . incessant, eternal, perpetual, continuous.

cross . . . . fretful, ill-tempered, crusty, ill-humoured.

cruelty . . . . . . oppression, tyranny, persecution.

dangerous . . . perilous, risky, hazardous.

dear . . . . expensive, costly.

decrease . . . . . curtail, reduce, diminish, contract, lessen.

difficult . . . . . hard, involved, intricate, unmanageable, perplexing.

disaster . . . . . misfortune, catastrophe, calamity, adversity.

discourse . . . . lecture, sermon, exhortation, dissertation.

disease . . . . . . malady, sickness, ailment.

disfigure . . . . . mar, deface, injure.

dishonest . . . . unjust, unfair, fraudulent, deceitful, deceptive, unscrupulous.

disorder . . . . . confusion, chaos.

dull . . . . dreary, gloomy, cheerless, lonesome, melancholy, backward.

eager . . . . keen, enthusiastic.

earn . . . . achieve, gain, win, merit, acquire.

ebb . . . . wane, decline, recede, sink, decay.

educate . . . . . train, guide, instruct, teach.

eject . . . . expel, dislodge, emit, cast.

elevate . . . . . . raise, lift, improve, heighten.

elude . . . . baffle, avoid, cheat, fool.

emancipate . . . free, liberate, loose, release.

embrace . . . . hug, clasp.

emotion . . . . . feeling, passion, tremor, agitation.

Synonyms (*contd.*)

enemy . . . . . . foe, adversary, opponent, antagonist.
enough . . . . . adequate, sufficient.
enquire . . . . . seek, search, investigate, pry, explore, trace, inspect, examine.
entice . . . . . . lure, persuade, allure.
entire. . . . . . . whole, total.
eradicate . . . . exterminate, eliminate, destroy.
esteem . . . . . . love, value, honour, prize, admire.
eternal. . . . . . perpetual, infinite, ceaseless.
exaggerate . . . magnify, heighten, enlarge, overstate, amplify.
excess . . . . . . surplus, increase.

famous . . . . . renowned, celebrated, eminent, distinguished.
fashion . . . . . custom, style, form.
fasten . . . . . . bind, tether, fix, join.
fatal . . . . deadly, mortal.
fate . . . . lot, destiny, end.
fault . . . . error, flaw, defect
fear . . . . terror, dread.
fearful . . . . . . timid, cowardly, frightened, faint-hearted, nervous.
fight . . . . battle, contest, combat, struggle, conflict, strife, contention.
firm. . . . . substantial, durable, lasting, binding.
float . . . . glide, drift, slip.
fond . . . . affectionate, loving, devoted.
frank. . . . . . . candid, outspoken, artless, open, sincere, plain, ingenuous.
friend . . . . . . comrade, companion, associate, colleague.
frugal . . . . . . thrifty, economical, sparing.
fruitful. . . . . . fertile, productive, luxuriant, prolific, fecund.

game . . . . pastime, recreation, sport, fun, frolic.
gay . . . . cheerful, merry, lively, jolly, blithe, buoyant.
gaze . . . . stare, espy, peer, reconnoitre.
general . . . . . universal, common.
generous . . . . liberal, big-hearted, noble.
genuine . . . . . pure, real.
good . . . . righteous, just, true, virtuous, upright.

habit . . . . custom, usage, way.
hateful. . . . . . abominable, detestable, execrable.
help. . . . . assist, aid, succour, support.
high . . . . tall, lofty, elaborate.
hinder . . . . . . obstruct, impede, thwart.
home. . . . . . . dwelling, residence, abode, habitation.

increase . . . . . enlarge, augment, amplify, multiply, extend, magnify, expand.

Synonyms (*contd.*)

infinite. . . . . . endless, eternal, everlasting, boundless, limitless.
injure . . . . . . hurt, harm, violate, wrong, ill-treat, damage.
insolvent . . . . bankrupt.
invasion. . . . . raid, attack.
invoke. . . . . . call, summon.
irritate. . . . . . tease, provoke.

kind . . . . thoughtful, considerate, tender, good, affectionate.

lazy. . . . . indolent, slothful, idle, inactive, sluggish, inert.
lure . . . . coax, entice, wheedle, persuade, inveigle, seduce, beguile.

map . . . . plan, design, outline, chart, sketch.
malice . . . . . . malevolence, spite, hate, rapacity.
merry . . . . . . gay, mirthful, jolly, sportive, joyous, jovial, jocund.
mistake . . . . . error, blunder, inaccuracy, fault.
motive. . . . . . reason, purpose.
mute . . . . dumb, silent.

narrate . . . . . tell, say, report, recite.
necessary . . . . needful, requisite, essential.
necessity . . . . want, need.

obey . . . . yield, submit.
obedient . . . . servile, cringing, submissive, meek, respectful.
oblation. . . . . gift, offering.
obscene . . . . . indecent, impure, vile.
odious. . . . . . offensive, hateful.
old . . . . ancient, antiquated, obsolete, antique.
omen. . . . . . . sign, foreboding, augury.
oral. . . . . verbal, unwritten.
oratory . . . . . eloquence, rhetoric.

pale. . . . . sallow, wan, pallid.
patron. . . . . . champion, advocate, supporter.
pitiful . . . . . . compassionate, sympathetic, consoling, piteous, merciful.
polite. . . . . . . affable, courteous, civil, obliging, polished, well-bred.
poor . . . . needy, destitute.
port. . . . . harbour, haven, shelter.
power . . . . . . ability, capacity, talent.
poverty . . . . . want, penury.
prattle . . . . . . chatter, jabber, gabble, gossip.
praise . . . . . . compliment, commend, applaud.
predict. . . . . . presage, herald, foretell.

Synonyms (*contd.*)

pretty . . . . . . beautiful, lovely, fine, attractive, handsome, neat, elegant, trim, gorgeous.

propagate . . . broadcast, advertise, proclaim, multiply, increase.

quiet . . . . calm, still, tranquil, serene, placid, peaceful.

rash. . . . . careless, tactless, indiscreet, reckless.

ready. . . . . . . prompt, alert, agile, nimble.

real . . . . authentic, genuine, original.

recruit . . . . . . tiro, novice, apprentice, amateur.

refugee . . . . . outlaw, fugitive, exile, outcast.

regent . . . . . . viceroy, deputy, substitute.

riot . . . . insurrection, revolt, mutiny, rising.

rude . . . . insolent, impolite, abusive, offensive.

rule . . . . govern, manage, supervise.

safe . . . . secure, sure, protected, locked, guarded.

scandal . . . . . slander, calumny.

scorn . . . . despise, abhor, condemn, deprecate.

see . . . . behold, perceive, discern, view, scan, descry.

silent . . . . reticent, taciturn, speechless.

sin. . . . . transgression, offence, misdemeanour.

sly. . . . . cunning, artful, crafty, subtle, shrewd, wily.

small . . . . tiny, puny, little.

smell . . . . scent, odour, perfume, fragrance.

smooth . . . . . level, plain, flat, uneven.

souvenir. . . . . memento, memorial, token, relic, remembrance.

speech . . . . . . eloquence, oratory, rhetoric.

spread . . . . . . scatter, disperse, distribute, disseminate, diffuse, broadcast.

stranger . . . . . foreigner, alien, immigrant.

strong . . . . . . powerful, muscular, robust, able, stalwart, sturdy, lusty.

suitable . . . . . appropriate, befitting, becoming.

surrender . . . . yield, relinquish, abandon, submit, capitulate.

timid . . . . cowardly, fearful, faint-hearted.

trick . . . . hoax.

trust . . . . rely, believe.

try. . . . . attempt, strive, endeavour, essay.

ugly. . . . . hideous, unsightly, horrid, uncouth, grotesque, squalid, repulsive.

value . . . . esteem, worth, appreciate, reverence.

victory. . . . . . success, triumph.

weak . . . . feeble, infirm, impotent, frail, flimsy.

HOMONYMS

Most examination papers in English language contain a question on the use of words of similar sound but different in meaning. The question usually takes a form something like the following:

Use these words in sentences to show that you know their meanings:

aisle	diary	principal	stationary	compliment
isle	dairy	principle	stationery	complement

A comprehensive list of these words is found in most good spelling books and it is not intended to repeat these here.

It is, however, important for the student to remember that when he is asked to use these words in sentences in order to illustrate their meaning, his sentences should be explicit enough as to leave no doubt in the examiner's mind that the writer knows the exact meaning of the words which he is using.

Take for example the words **stationary, stationery.** When used in the following sentences the meaning is not fully brought out.

(a) The bus is **stationary**. (b) I bought some **stationery** at the store.

Sentences (c) and (d) however, leave no doubt in the reader's mind that the writer is fully acquainted with the meaning of the words:

(c) Wait until the bus is <u>**stationary**</u> before attempting to get off.

(d) I will need a good deal of <u>**stationery**</u> to write all these letters.

Note also that it is a good plan to underline the significant word in the sentence.

DISTINCTIVE SOUNDS

hens	cluck, cackle, chuckle	wolves	howl
geese	cackle	sparrows	chirp
ducks	quack	crickets	chirp
turkeys	gobble	robins	chirp
parrots	chatter	hounds	bay
monkeys	chatter	sheep, goat, calf	bleat
frogs	croak	elephants	trumpet
ravens	croak	lions	roar
rooks	caw	bitterns	boom
crows	caw	snakes	hiss
dogs	howl, growl, snarl, bark	serpents	hiss

Distinctive sounds (*contd.*)

owls . . . . hoot, screech, cur	swashing of the sea
cats . . . . mew, purr	swishing of ladies' skirts
bulls . . . . bellow	hooting of a steam whistle
oxen . . . . low	tooting of a horn
cows . . . . moo	screeching of brakes
grasshoppers . . . . chirr	roaring, rolling, rumbling of thunder
apes . . . . gibber	rumbling of heavy vehicles
bears . . . . growl	whizzing of arrows
eagles . . . . scream	buzzing of a telephone
hyenas . . . . laugh, scream	zooming of aeroplanes
seagulls . . . . scream	crackling of fire, wood, dry leaves
bees . . . . buzz	tinkling of coins
beetles . . . . drone	popping of corks
rabbits . . . . squeal	tinkling of glasses
pigs . . . . grunt, squeal	tinkling of bells
wrens . . . . warble	jingling, chiming of bells
doves . . . . coo	shuffling of feet
swallows . . . . twitter	whirring of wings
mice . . . . squeak	crinkling of paper
deer . . . . bell	clangour of hammers
asses . . . . bray	clanking of chains
horses . . . . neigh, whinny	ticking of a clock
	clatter of horses' hoofs
howling of the wind	creaking of hinges
pattering of the rain	hissing of steam
gurgling of the rivers	rustle of silk or leaves
babbling of the brooks	crack of a whip
splashing of water	
lapping of water	

DISTINCTIVE NAMES GIVEN TO THE YOUNG OF ANIMALS

Adult	Young
cat	kitten
cock	cockerel
cow	calf
horse	foal
ass	foal
sheep	lamb

Distinctive names given to the young of animals (*contd.*)

hen	pullet
cow	heifer (one that has not yet given birth to a calf)
bull	calf
deer	fawn
dog	puppy
duck	duckling
pig	piglet
eagle	eaglet
owl	owlet
fowl	chicken
goat	kid
goose	gosling
stallion (horse)	colt or foal
mare	filly
hare	leveret
frog (toad)	tadpole
trout	fry
salmon	parr
bird	nestling
hawk	bowet
eel	elver
lion, bear, fox	cub
butterfly, moth	caterpillar
swan	cygnet

Diminutives

With these may be grouped the following diminutives formed from:

animal ...	animalcule, animalculum	flower	floweret
ball	ballet, bullet	fourth	farthing
brace	bracelet	globe	globule
cask	casket	grain	granule
convent	conventicle	hill	hillock
corn	kernel	ice	icicle
cover	coverlet	isle	islet
crown	coronet	lance	lancet
dear	darling	lass	lassie
eagle	eaglet	latch	latchet

Diminutives (contd.)

leaf	leaflet	sack	satchel
lock	locket	scythe	sickle
man	manikin, mannikin	seed	seedlet
park	paddock	sphere	spherule
part	particle	stream	streamlet
ring	ringlet	tower	turret
river	rivulet	verse	versicle, verselet, verset

DISTINCTIVE ADJECTIVES CONNECTED WITH CERTAIN WORDS

Pertaining to—

goats	caprine
eagle	aquiline
horses	equine, callavine, equestrian
lion	leonine
hares	leporine
wolf	lupine
peacock	pavonine
pigeons	peristeronic
fish	piscine
parrots	psittaceous
fox	vulpine
swine, pigs	porcine
cats	feline
goose	anserine
ships or sailors	nautical
ships	naval
spring	vernal
winter	brumal
autumn	autumnal
birth	natal
mother	maternal
father	paternal
sister	sororal
brother	fraternal
uncle	avuncular
duke	ducal
son or daughter	filial
serpent	serpentine

Pertaining to—

infant	infantile
servant	menial
shepherds	pastoral, bucolic
priests	sacerdotal
priesthood	hieratic
author	auctorial
tailor	sartorial
barber	tonsorial
wife	uxorial
day	diurnal
morning	matinal
evening	vesper
night	nocturnal
marriage	connubial, nuptial
matrimony	conjugal
love	erotic
heaven	celestial
earth	terrestrial
asses	asinine
bees	apiarian
cattle	bovine
dogs	canine
sheep	ovine
crow	corvine
wild beasts	ferine
smelling	olfactory
seeing	visual, optical
dinner	prandial
hearing	auditory, aural

Distinctive adjectives connected with certain words (*contd.*)

Pertaining to—		*Pertaining to—*	
sound	acoustic	dancing	terpsichorean
water	aquatic	weaving	textile
air	pneumatic	fishing	piscatory
rain	pluvial	swimming	natatory
sea	maritime, marine	first age	primeval
belly	alvine	old age	senile
brain	cerebral	fats	sebaceous, adipose
heart	cardiac	moon	lunar
breast or chest	pectoral	stars	astral, sidereal, stellar
iron	ferrous	sun	solar
tin	stannic	land	praedial
silk	sericate	gums	gingival
river	fluvial	tongue	glossal
leaves	foliar	throat	guttural
rope	funicular	lips	labial
island	insular	hair	crinal
tears	lachrymal	nose	nasal
milk	lacteal	floods	diluvial
lamp	lucermal	parish	parochial
country	rural, rustic	lungs	pulmonary
town or city	urban	The Apostle Peter	Petrine
money	monetary, pecuniary, fiscal	The Apostle Paul	Pauline
coins	numismatic	Bernard Shaw	Shavian
preaching	predicatory	Oxford University	Oxonian
colour	chromatic	Cambridge University	Cantabrigian
kitchen	culinary	Canterbury	Cantuarian
law court	forensic	Alps	Alpine

WORDS FREQUENTLY MISSPELT

(Arranged in groups of ten words—for rapid revision)

(1)	(2)	(3)	(4)	(5)
until	pursue	ceiling	diarrhoea	chauffeur
separate	pursuer	receive	dysentery	superintendent
ninety	pursuit	receipt	diphtheria	secretary
psalm	sanctify	niece	typhoid	lieutenant
psalmist	sanctity	sieve	tuberculosis	oculist
psalter	khaki	yield	diary	sepulchre
arctic	bouquet	February	dairy	cemetery
antarctic	ecstasy	Wednesday	eight	symmetry
asthma	privilege	bicycle	gramophone	dying
dipthong	hiccough	cedar	mortgage	dyeing

Words frequently misspelt (*contd.*)

(6)	(7)	(8)	(9)	(10)
conceit	benefit	adjacent	haemorrhage	neighbour
deceive	benefiting	embalm	paralysis	plumber
thief	begin	debtor	pneumonia	quay
bier	beginning	condemn	pneumatic	disciple
handerkerchief	accommodate	buoyant	catarrh	martyr
hygiene	eczema	diaphragm	dungeon	mischief
geography	phlegm	liquor	veil	mischievous
grammar	abscess	anxious	sceptre	restaurant
chasm	yacht	anxiety	aisle	chaos
truly	forty	recipe	subtle	committee

(11)	(12)	(13)	(14)	(15)
bailiff	commercial	curiosity	encyclopedia	aide-de-camp
recipe	vicious	muscles	rhythm	chassis
physician	abyss	reservoir	syringe	camouflage
yolk	abysmal	zephyr	soliloquy	ballet
viscount	almighty	mosquito	picnic	depot
wrestle	character	knuckle	picnicking	gauge
borough	manoeuvre	resign	pavilion	amateur
gnaw	teetotaller	knowledge	bazaar	bureau
islet	jubilee	rheumatism	gaiety	buffet
lightning	avoirdupois	library	luscious	bayonet

(16)	(17)	(18)	(19)	(20)
bulletin	champagne	queue	apostle	seize
biscuit	psychology	sergeant	catechism	relieve
scythe	coupon	plague	schism	believe
synonym	rogue	matinee	hymn	suite
fatigue	auxiliary	rendezvous	chorus	fashion
gnat	autumn	connoisseur	choir	athlete
debris	kiln	debt	myrrh	campaign
debt	sceptre	solumn	dependent	influenza
sovereign	centre	etiquette	dependant	spasm
exaggerate	moustache	guitar	wholly	shield

(21)	(22)	(23)	(24)	(25)
heifer	pianos	agreeable	audible	abundance
colonel	solos	noticeable	edible	correspondence
kernel	tomatoes	movable	visible	independence
design	photos	notable	available	occurrence
foreign	mottoes	marriageable	digestible	existence
victuals	potatoes	valuable	forcible	acquaintance
neigh	banjoes	changeable	preventable	maintain
pageant	dynamos	advisable	inevitable	maintenance
viscount	manifestos	pleasurable	inseparable	impertinence
maize	mulattos	excusable	responsible	permanence

Words frequently misspelt (*contd.*)

(26)	(27)	(28)	(29)	(30)
preliminary	apparatus	motor	commissioner	advice
sorcery	analyse	persecutor	photographer	advise
physical	hoeing	prosecutor	luggage	practice
sustain	honour	operator	confectioner	practise
sustenance	honourable	donor	aviator	council
cashier	honorary	refrigerator	altar	counsel
column	humour	sculptor	alter	licence
besiege	favour	surveyor	calibre	license
unique	favourite	supervisor	sombre	stationery
believe	councillor	coroner	centre	stationary

(31)	(32)	(33)	(34)	(35)
parallel	singe	zinc	plough	realm
puncheon	singeing	rein	mileage	disease
parcel	wharf	reign	fulfil	decease
pencil	counterfeit	skein	install	bankrupt
freight	geology	envelope	gallop	jealousy
courtesy	grieve	enthusiasm	galloping	hypocrite
Britain	patience	corpse	judgment	ankle
extinct	weight	corps	belfry	piece
persuade	tongs	copse	eruption	doze
spectre	tongues	caustic	irruption	dose

(36)	(37)	38)	(39)	(40)
abbreviation	opponent	earnest	surety	gaol
accumulate	opportunity	punctual	martial	goal
battalion	perennial	punctuality	height	peasant
buccaneer	programme	thorough	deceive	tincture
colonnade	rebellion	luscious	principal	chaplain
recommend	association	skilful	principle	surgeon
ellipse	woollen	heinous	sign	malicious
embarrass	wholly	currant	business	dough
harass	possession	current	sculptor	villain
lettuce	leisure	chronic	discern	debtor

(41)	(42)	(43)	(44)	(45)
vein	parasol	tough	enough	canoe
siege	fibre	calibre	curtain	lyre
overwhelm	fulfil	course	heir	shrewd
cavalier	hearse	coarse	heiress	syllabus
instinct	shrewd	thigh	vault	lair
critic	alms	czar (tsar)	juice	liar
criticism	theatre	czarina	physique	sauce
atmosphere	brief	mosque	phenomenon	appendix
stalk	their	spectacle	gigantic	hippopotamus
colour	measles	puncture	sphere	memorandum

Words frequently misspelt (*contd.*)

(46)	(47)	(48)	(49)	(50)
portmanteau	tariff	pharmacy	wilful	trophy
radius	sabre	secrecy	social	trousers
plateau	adieu	icicle	cathedral	eucharist
Mediterranean	pronounce	laundry	hydraulic	usury
Shakespeare	pronunciation	sacrifice	ascension	medicine
altogether	technical	logarithm	cocoa	mechanic
development	laughter	eclipse	conscience	grotesque
career	anecdote	science	tarpaulin	picturesque
focus	chalice	stratagem	instalment	umbrella
ladle	phantasy	tragedy	eccentric	embezzle

GENERAL KNOWLEDGE

DISTINCTIVE NAMES GIVEN TO SOME COUNTRIES

The Emerald Isle	Ireland
Hibernia	Ireland
The Pearl of the Antilles	Cuba
The Magnificent Province	Guyana
The Land of Oat Cakes	Scotland
The Land of the Golden Fleece	Australia
The Land of the Midnight Sun	Lapland, Norway
The Land of the Flying Fish	Barbados
The Land of the Eucalyptus	Australasia
The Land of the Rising Sun	Japan
The Land of the Five Rivers	Punjab, in Pakistan and India
The Land of the Humming-bird	Trinidad
The Land of the Dykes	Holland
The Land of the Tulips	Holland
The Land of Milk and Honey	Canaan
The Land of the White Elephant	Thailand
The Land of the Thousand Lakes	Finland
The Sugar Mill of the Antilles	Cuba
The Isle of Springs	Jamaica
The Barbary States	Morocco, Algeria, Tunisia and Libya
The Granary of Spain	Andalusia
The Spice Islands	Moluccas in the East Indies
The mother-in-law of Europe	Denmark

Distinctive names given to some countries (*contd.*)

Our Lady of Snow	Canada
The bread basket of the Empire	Canada
The spice island of the west	Grenada
The roof of the world	Tibet
The white man's grave	West Africa
The sea of mountains	British Columbia
The Iberian Peninsula	Spain and Portugal
The Promised Land	Canaan
The battle-field of Europe	Belgium
The playground of Europe	Switzerland
The Antipodes	New Zealand
The George Cross Island	Malta
Little Venice	Venezuela
Rich Coast	Costa Rica
Rich Port	Puerto Rico
The dairy of Northern Europe	Denmark
Caledonia	Scotland
The sick man of Europe	The Turkish Empire
The halfway house of the Pacific	Hawaii
Robinson Crusoe's Island	Juan Fernandez, Tobago
Mountainous Country	Haiti
The Celestial Empire	China
The Land of Han	China
The saw mill of Europe	Sweden
The mother colony of the West Indies	St Kitts
The Gift of the Nile	Egypt
The storehouse of the world	Mexico
The island of the hawks	Azores
Everglade State	Florida
Holy Land	Palestine

DISTINCTIVE NAMES GIVEN TO
SOME TOWNS

The Garden of England	County of Kent
County Palatine	Lancashire

Distinctive names given to some towns (*contd.*)

The Garden State	New Jersey
The Golden State	California
The Silver State	Nevada
The Copper State	Arizona
Blue Hen State	Delaware
The Nutmeg State	Connecticut
Garden of America	Virginia
Old Dominion	Virginia
The Eternal City	Rome
The twin city	Budapest
The Imperial City	Rome
The Holy City	Jerusalem
The Holy City of the Hindus	Benares
The Golden City	Johannesburg
The Diamond City	Kimberley
Windy City	Chicago
The twin cities of the Mississippi	St Paul and Minneapolis
The city of magnificent distances	Washington, D.C.
The automobile capital of the world	Detroit
The meat market of the world	Chicago
The mother city of Russia	Kiev
The city of the Arabian nights	Baghdad
The Birmingham of Belgium	Liège
The Paris of the East	Bucharest
City of Pleasure	Bucharest
The hub of the Universe	Boston
The modern Babylon	London
The Liverpool of France	Le Havre
The City of God	Allahabad
The Queen of the Adriatic	Venice
The lighthouse of the Mediterranean	Stromboli
An ice-house in winter and a furnace in summer	Madrid
The Manchester of France	Rouen
The Manchester of Poland	Lodz
The Gibraltar of the North	Sveaborg, near Helsingfors
The Iron Gates	The deep gorge of the Danube, near Orsova, in Rumania
The Gibraltar of the Pacific	Corregidor
The Pearl of the Orient	Damascus

Distinctive names given to some towns (*contd.*)

Valley of Kings	Thebes
Athens of the West	Leyden
Gibraltar of America	Quebec
City of Elms	New Haven
Queen City	Regina, Cincinnati
The eye of Greece	Athens
The Rome of the Ocean, the Bride of the Sea	Venice
The Athens of the North	Edinburgh

DISTINCTIVE NAMES GIVEN TO SOME FAMOUS MEN AND WOMEN

Many famous men and women in history have been called by distinctive names. Here is a list of of some of them:

The Great Commoner	William Pitt, the elder
The Iron Duke	The Duke of Wellington
The Grand Old Man	William Ewart Gladstone
The wisest fool in Christendom	King James I of England
The Bard of Avon	William Shakespeare
The Blind Poet	John Milton
The Iron Chancellor	Prince Otto Von Bismarck
The Old Pilot	Prince Otto Von Bismarck
The Little Corporal	Napoleon Bonaparte
The Black Napoleon	Jean Jacques Dessalines, of Haiti
The Beloved Disciple	St John
The Apostle of the Indians	Bartholome de Las Cassa
The Black Prince	Son of Edward III, King of England
Cœur de Lion	Richard I of England
Farmer George	King George III of England
The Merrie Monarch	King Charles II of England
The Light of Asia	Buddha
The Mad Monk	Rasputin
The Dickens of France	Honoré de Balzac
The Sage of Concord	Ralph Waldo Emerson
The Sailor King	King William IV of England
The First Gentleman in Europe	King George IV of England

Distinctive names given to some famous men and women (*contd.*)

The head of the Buddhist faith in Tibet	Dalai Lama
The Unready	King Ethelred II of England
Longshanks	Edward I of England
Edward the Peacemaker	Edward VII of England
The King Maker	Richard Neville, Earl of Warwick
Thorough	Thomas Wentworth, Earl of Strafford
Old Rough and Ready	Zachary Taylor, a President of the USA
Old Dreadnought	The English Admiral, Boscawen
The Morning Star of the Reformation	John Wycliff
Lawrence of Arabia	Col Thomas Edward Lawrence
The Swedish Nightingale	Jenny Lind
William the Conqueror	William I of England
The Maid of Norway	Daughter of Eric II, King of Norway
The Lady of the Lamp	Florence Nightingale
The Virgin Queen	Queen Elizabeth I
The Maid of Orleans	Joan of Arc
Madonna	The Virgin Mary
The Holy Father, His Holiness	The Pope
The Apostle of Northumbria	Saint Aidan
Mata Hari	Marguerite Gertrude, a spy
The Laughing Philosopher	Democritus
The Grand Old Man of Hungary	Count Albert Apponyi
The Faultless Painter	Andrea del Sarto
The Learned Blacksmith	Elihu Burritt, an American linguist
The Young Pretender	Charles Edward Stuart, grandson of James II of England
The most musical of all Englishmen	Sir William Sterndale Bennett
The Seraphic Doctor	St Bonaventura
The Semiramis of the North	Catherine II, Empress of Russia
Defender of the Holy Sepulchre	Godfrey of Bouillon
The Inspired Idiot	Oliver Goldsmith
Noll	Oliver Cromwell
The Magnificent	Sultan Solyman
The Uncrowned Queen of Arabia	Gertrude Bell

With these may also be classed the following:

The Father of Poets	Homer
The Father of English Poetry	Geoffrey Chaucer

Distinctive names given to some famous men and women (*contd.*)

The Father of Biography	Plutarch
The Father of History	Herodotus
The Father of Experimental Philosophy	Francis Bacon
The Father of Moral Philosophy	Thomas Aquinas
The Father of Medicine	Hippocrates
The Father of Modern Astronomy	Copernicus
The Father of Modern Chemistry	Antoine Lavoisier
The Father of Natural History	John Ray
The Father of the Science of Political Economy	Adam Smith
The Father of Unitarianism	John Biddle
The Father of Modern Music	Johann Sebastian Bach
The Father of Novel Writing	Giovanni Boccaccio

OTHER DISTINCTIVE NAMES OF PERSONS, PLACES AND THINGS

The Gilded Chamber	The House of Lords
The Vatican	The home of the Pope in Rome
The White House	The home of the President of USA
No. 10 Downing Street	The home of the Prime Minister of Britain
The Citadel of Athens	The Acropolis
The Colosseum	The ruins of the Flavian amphitheatre in Rome
The Alhambra	The famous palace and stronghold of the Moorish kings of Granada in Spain
Fleet Street	The newspaper centre of Britain
Wall Street	The financial centre of USA
The Pillars of Hercules	Two great rocks, Gibraltar and Ceuta, commanding the entrance to the Mediterranean Sea
Indian corn	Maize
Indian date	Tamarind
Indian file	Single file, *i.e.* one person walking behind the other
Paternoster	The Lord's Prayer
Chanticleer	A cock
Potter's field	A burial ground for the very poor and unknown

Other distinctive names of persons, places and things (*contd.*)

Persian apple	The peach
Adam's apple	The larynx
Adam's ale	Water
The inner man	The stomach
Junker	A member of the German aristocracy
Limb of the Law	Policeman
Kulak	A Russian land-owning peasant
The silver streak	The English Channel
Black art	Witchcraft
The herring pond	The Atlantic Ocean
The House of Keys	Parliament of the Isle of Man
Iron horse	A train
The gentle craft	Shoemaking
The lamp of Heaven	The moon
The universal arithmetic	Algebra
China's sorrow	The Hwang-Ho
River of Silver	Rio-de-la-Plata
Quicksilver	mercury
The garden of France	The Loire Valley
Black diamond	Coal
Capital punishment	The death sentence
The Ashes	Symbol of victory in international cricket matches
King of metals	Gold
God's acre	A churchyard
God's image	The human body
A Good Samaritan	A friend in need
Bottomless pit	Hell
White plague	Tuberculosis
Hansen's disease	leprosy
White fuel	Water power
April gentleman	A newly-married man
Scotland Yard	The headquarters of the London Metropolitan Police Force
Old Bailey	The Central Criminal Court in London, England
The Father of the waters	The River Nile
King of the waters	The River Amazon
King of the jungle	The tiger
King of beasts	The lion

Other distinctive names of persons, places and things (*contd.*)

King of the sea	The herring
Sheep's eyes	Looks of love
Bird of peace	The dove
The olive branch	A symbol of peace
Morganatic marriage	Marriage of a king or queen or one of royal rank to one of a lower rank
The head of the Roman Catholic Church	The Pope
The head of the Church of England	The Queen and then the Archbishop of Canterbury
Bird of Jove	The eagle
Bird of Juno	The peacock
Bird of night	The owl
American leopard	The jaguar
John Bull	An Englishman
Cockney	A Londoner
The fourth estate	The Press
The sinews of war	Money
Gentlemen of the robe	The legal profession
The sterner sex	Men
The fairer sex	Women
Flower of the flock	The best child of a family
Land of the Leal	Heaven
Lent Lily	The daffodil
Ocean greyhound	A swift ship
House of correction	A prison, penitentiary
A man of letters	A scholarly author
Jack Tar	A seaman
Mother tongue	one's native language
Baker's dozen	thirteen

GREAT INVENTIONS

Alexander Graham Bell	The telephone
Thomas Alva Edison	The phonograph
E. Berliner	The gramophone
Professor David Edward Hughes	The microphone

Great inventions (*contd.*)

John L. Baird	Television
Evangelista Torricelli	The barometer
Galileo Galilei	The thermometer and the telescope
Janssen	The microscope
William Gascoigne	The micrometer
John Harrison	The chronometer
Laennec	The stethoscope
Sir David Brewster	The kaleidoscope
Orville and Wilbur Wright	The aeroplane
Count Von Ferdinand Zeppelin	The Zeppelin dirigible airship
Dr Alfred Bernhard Nobel	Dynamite
Roger Bacon	Gunpowder
Sir Hiram Stevens Maxim	The automatic gun
Samuel Colt	The revolver
Sir Joseph Whitworth	The Whitworth rifle
Elias Howe	The sewing-machine
James Watt	The steam engine
George Stephenson	The locomotive
James Nasmyth	The steam hammer
Sir Charles Algernon Parsons	The steam turbine
Marchese Gulielmo Marconi	The wireless telegraph
Michael Faraday	The dynamo and electric transformer
Messrs Coke and Wheatstone	The electric telegraph
Benjamin Franklin	The lightning conductor
Robert Stephenson	The flashing system of throwing light out to sea from lighthouses
Sir Humphry Davy	The safety lamp
Sir Joseph Wilson Swan	The incandescent electric lamp
	The autotype process of photography
	The art of making rapid dry photographic plates
George Eastman	The roll photographic film
	The Kodak camera
Alois Senefelder	Lithography
Johann Gutenberg	The art of printing
Ludwig Lazarus Zamenhof	Esperanto
Samuel Finley Morse	The Morse Code of signals
	The Morse system of electric telegraph
Gerhardus Mercator	A celestial and a terrestrial globe

Great Inventions (*contd.*)

Sir Richard Arkwright	The spinning frame
Edmund Cartwright	The power loom
Samuel Crompton	The spining mule
James Hargreaves	The spinning jenny
Sir Henry Bessemer	The process of converting cast-iron into steel
John Macadam	Macadamised roads
Henry Cort	The process known as "puddling" for converting pig iron into malleable iron
The Marquis De Vauban	Income tax

FAMOUS DISCOVERERS, NAVIGATORS, EXPLORERS AND INVENTORS

Christopher Columbus discovered or re-discovered	America, and the W. Indies
Vasco Nunez de Balboa discovered	The Pacific Ocean
Sir Humphrey Gilbert discovered	Newfoundland
Vasco Da Gama discovered	The sea route to India 1498
Sebastian Cabot discovered	Labrador in 1497
Captain James Cook discovered	The Sandwich Isles
Henry, the Navigator discovered	Madeira and the Azores

Henry Hudson discovered Hudson River, Hudson Strait, Hudson Bay

Ferdinand Magellan was the first person to attempt to sail around the world.

Sir Francis Drake was the first Englishman to sail around the world, 1577-1580.

William Baffin discovered Baffin Bay.

Sir Martin Frobisher discovered Frobisher's Strait.

Matthew Flinders discovered Bass Strait.

Vitus Bering discovered Bering's Strait.

John Davis discovered Davis Strait.

Famous discoverers, navigators, explorers and inventors (*contd.*)

Sir Samuel White Baker discovered Lake Albert in 1864.

Marco Polo made explorations in China, India and the East.

Captain Roald Amundsen reached the South Pole in 1912; flew over the North Pole in 1926.

Rear Admiral Richard Evelyn Byrd flew over the North Pole in 1926; flew over the South Pole in 1929.

Rear Admiral Robert Edwin Peary succeeded in reaching the North Pole on 6 April, 1909.

Captain Robert Scott reached the South Pole, 18 January, 1912.

David Livingstone explored a great deal of Central Africa between 1849 and 1873.

Sir Henry Morton Stanley explored Central Africa between 1871 and 1889.

Mungo Park explored the River Niger 1795-1806.

Jacques Cartier explored a great deal of Canada, especially the Gulf of St Lawrence and the river St Lawrence.

Charles Goodyear discovered the art of vulcanising rubber.

Professor Pierre Curie and Madame Curie were the joint discoverers of Radium, a substance used in the cure of cancer.

Edward Jenner discovered vaccination.

Lord Lister discovered antiseptic treatment.

Robert Koch discovered the bacillus of tuberculosis.

William Harvey discovered the circulation of the blood.

Louis Pasteur discovered the science of bacteria, *i.e.* the germ-theory of diseases.

Professor Wilhelm Konrad Rontgen discovered Rontgen rays (X-rays).

Sir James Young Simpson discovered the use of chloroform as an anaesthetic.

William Hyde Wollaston discovered ultra-violet rays.

Joseph Priestley discovered oxygen.

Sir William Ramsay discovered argon gas and helium.

Sir Ronald Ross discovered the cause of malaria.

Sir Patrick Manson discovered that the malarial parasite was transmitted by the anopheles mosquito.

Sir Aldo Castellani discovered the cause of sleeping sickness.

Sir Isaac Newton discovered the law of gravitation.

Henry Cavendish discovered the composition of water; he also discovered hydrogen.

Famous discoverers, navigators, explorers and inventors (*contd.*)

Francis Appert discovered how to preserve animal and vegetable food by enclosing them in hermetically sealed tins or cans.

Archimedes discovered specific gravity and the principles of the lever.

Bernard Pallisy discovered the art of producing white enamel.

Sir Rowland Hill introduced the penny postal system.

William Herschel discovered the planet Uranus.

Sir Alexander Fleming discovered penicillin.

FAMOUS FOUNDERS

Lord Robert Baden-Powell founded the Boy Scouts in 1908.

"General" William Booth founded The Salvation Army, in 1878.

John Wesley was the founder of the "Methodist" church.

Sir George Williams, founder of the Young Men's Christian Association (Y.M.C.A.).

Mrs Mary Baker Eddy founded the Christian Science religion.

St Benedict, founder of the Order of Benedictine Monks.

Jeremy Bentham, founder of the Utilitarian school of philosophy.

Professor Alfred Adler, founder of the school of Individual Psychology.

Confucius, founder of Chinese Philosophy.

Dr Sun Yat Sen, founder of the Chinese Republic.

William Penn, founder of Pennsylvania, in 1682.

Sir Thomas Raffles founded Singapore in 1819.

Diego Velasquez founded Santiago and Havana.

Dr Thomas John Barnado founded the homes for orphan-waifs, which bear his name.

Friedrich Wilhelm Froebel, founder of the Kindergarten system of education.

Sir Isaac Pitman found the Pitman system of Shorthand.

Sir Francis Galton founded the study of Eugenics.

Friedrich Anton Mesmer founded the system of Mesmerism.

Alfred Krupp founded the great gun factories at Essen, Germany, which were the largest in the world.

Joseph Smith, founder of the religious sect called Mormons.

Sir William Smith founded the Boys' Brigade in 1883

PIONEERS

The first persons to fly across the Atlantic
                    Sir John Alcock and Sir A. Whitten Brown in 1919
The first person to fly from England to New Zealand
                                        Jean Gardner Batten
The first person to fly the English Channel from Calais to Dover
                                        Louis Bleriot
The first person to fly in Great Britain   William Cody in 1908
The first solo Atlantic flight   Charles Lindbergh, May 1927
The first woman to fly the Atlantic   Amelia Earhart, June 1928
The first woman to fly solo from England to Australia
                                        Amy Johnson
The first person to cross Africa from east to west
                                        Verney L. Cameron
The first person to take a successful photograph of the human face
                                        John William Draper
The first Socialist to be elected to the House of Commons
                                        James Keir Hardie
The first mountaineers to reach the top of Mount Everest
                    Sherpa Tensing and Sir Edmund Hillary
The first man to travel in space   Yuri Gagarin, April 1961
The first man to walk on the moon   Neil Armstrong, July 1969

SOME RECORD HOLDERS

The largest church in the world   Saint Peter's in Rome
The tallest building in the world   Empire State Building
                                New York City, USA, 442 m high
The longest bridge in the world

                                Lower Zambesi, Africa, 3541 metres
The largest bird in the world   The ostrich
The lightest of all substances   Hydrogen gas

SOME FAMOUS EDUCATIONISTS

Friedrich Wilhelm Froebel
Maria Montessori
Johann Pestalozzi
John Dewey
Francisco Ferrer

Robert Raikes
Archbishop Cranmer
Elizabeth Fry
John Howard
Jean Piaget

SOME FAMOUS RELIGIOUS REFORMERS

John Huss
Hugh Latimer
Ulrich Zwingli

Martin Luther
John Wesley
John Calvin

SOME FAMOUS PHILANTHROPISTS

Andrew Carnegie
George Cadbury
John Howard
Baron Maurice de Hirsch
Viscount Nuffield

Julia Ward Howe
Robert Owen
John D. Rockefeller
Rabindranath Tagore
Dr Alfred Nobel

MYTHOLOGY

Muses: The Muses were the goddesses who presided over the liberal arts. There were nine muses, as follows:
Clio, the muse of history; *Calliope*, the muse of epic poetry; *Euterpe*, the muse of lyric poetry; *Erato*, the muse of love poetry; *Melpomene*, the muse of tragedy; *Thalia*, the muse of comedy; *Urania,* the muse of astronomy; *Terpsichore*, the muse of dancing; and *Polyhymnia*, the muse of psalmody or religious song.

Graces: The Graces were three goddesses representing the perfection of beauty and charm. They were *Algaia, Euphrosyne* and *Thalia.*

GODS AND GODDESSES

The god of		*The goddess of*	
War	Mars	Peace	Pax
Wine	Bacchus	Vengeance	Nemesis
Riches	Plutus	Fruit	Pomena
Fertility	Priapus	Morning	Aurora
The Sea	Neptune	Fire	Vesta
Heaven	Uranus	Hunting	Diana
Fire	Vulcan	Wisdom	Minerva
Medicine	Apollo	War	Minerva
Music	Apollo	The Liberal Arts	Minerva
Day	Apollo	Love	Venus
The Underworld	Pluto	The Hearth	Vesta
Healing	Aesculapius	The Earth	Rhea
Flocks and Herds	Apollo	The earth's produce	Ceres
Protection and Punishment	Apollo	Justice	Astraea
The Rivers	Alpheus	Infatuation	Ate
Revelry and Feasting	Comus	War	Bellona
Love	Cupid	Chastity	Bona Dea
The Sun	Sol or Helius, Baal	Silence	Calypso
Marriage	Hymen	Flowers	Flora
Sleep and Dreams	Morpheus	Law and Justice	Themis
Sleep	Somus	Health	Hygeia
Shepherds and Hunters	Pan		
The water which surrounded the earth	Oceanus		

WEDDING ANNIVERSARIES

Wedding Anniversaries are social events. Here is a complete list of Wedding Anniversaries appropriately named. Those not named are usually giftless Anniversaries. Gifts presented to the celebrating couple by their friends are usually made of materials corresponding to the name of the Anniversary.

1st year—Paper		8th year—Bronze	
2nd year—Calico		9th year—Pottery	
3rd year—Leather		10th year—Tin	
4th year—Silk or Book, Fruit or Flowers		11th year—Steel	
5th year—Wood		12th year—Linen	
6th year—Iron		13th year—Lace	
7th year—Copper or Brass		14th year—Ivory	
		15th year—Crystal	

Wedding anniversaries (*contd.*)

20th year—Chinaware
25th year—SILVER WEDDING ANNIVERSARY
30th year—Pearls
35th year—Coral and Jade
40th year—Ruby
45th year—Sapphire
50th year—GOLDEN WEDDING ANNIVERSARY
55th year—Emerald
60th year—DIAMOND WEDDING ANNIVERSARY

COINS USED IN DIFFERENT COUNTRIES

Balboa	Panama
Bolivar	Venezuela
Colon	Costa Rica, El Salvador
Cordoba	Nicaragua
Cruzeiro	Brazil
Deutsche Mark	Germany
Dinar	Yugoslavia, Iraq
Dollar	Australia, USA, Canada, China. Malaysia, Hong Kong
Drachma	Greece
Escudo	Portugal
Forint	Hungary
Franc	France, Belgium, Luxembourg, Switzerland, Albania
Gourde	Haiti
Guilder	Netherlands
Koruna	Czechoslovakia
Krone	Denmark, Norway, Sweden
Kyat	Burma
Lempira	Honduras
Lev	Bulgaria, Rumania
Lira	Italy
Marka	Finland
Naira	Nigeria
Peso	Various Latin American countries, notably Mexico
£ Sterling	United Kingdom, Eire, New Zealand
Rail	Iran
Rand	South Africa
Rouble	USSR
Rupee	Pakistan, India, Sri Lanka
Schilling	Austria
Sol	Peru
Sucre	Ecuador
Yen	Japan
Zloty	Poland

RELIGION

The Decalogue	The Ten Commandments.
Koran	The sacred scriptures of Islam.
Apocrypha	A collection of fourteen books of the Old Testament, not considered genuine by the Jews. The Protestant Churches regard the Apocrypha only as historical records, and it is not included in the authorized version of the Bible. Some of the Books included 1 and 2 Esdras, Tobit, Judith, Esther X-XVI, etc.
Apocalypse	The book of the New Testament in which the revelation of St John is recorded.
Apocalyptic Number	The mystical number 666 which is mentioned in the Apocalypse.
Canticles	The songs of Solomon.
The Major Prophets	Jeremiah, Ezekiel, Daniel, Isaiah.
Pentateuch	The first five books of the Old Testament, namely, Genesis, Exodus, Leviticus, Numbers and Deuteronomy.
The Golden Rule	"Do unto others as you would have others do unto you."
Bhagavad-Gita	Hindu sacred scriptures.
Paternoster	The Lord's Prayer.
Cardinal or Seven deadly sins	Pride, lust, envy, anger, covetousness, gluttony, and sloth.
Millennium	The thousand years, according to Revelations 20: 1–5 during which Jesus Christ will rule the world.

SOME PATRON SAINTS

St. George of England, St. Andrew of Scotland, St. Patrick of
Ireland, St. David of Wales, St. James of Spain, St. Dennis of
France, St. Anthony of Italy, St. Nicholas of Russia, St. Cecilia
of Music, St. Crispin of Shoemakers, St. Pancras of Children, St.
Christopher of Travellers.

SOME LOCAL NAMES GIVEN TO CERTAIN PLANTS AND ANIMALS

Local Name	English Name	Local Name	English Name
Ochroes	Ladies' Finger	Roucou	Annatto
Sour Orange	Seville Orange	Jumbie Bead	Coral Bean
Chataigne	Breadnut	Pewah	Peachnut
Caimite	Star Apple	Manicou	Opossum
Pomme		Pak Choi	Chinese
Cythere	Golden Apple	Pe Ts-ai	Cabbage
Zabocca	Avocado	Crapaud	Crabwood
Pimento		Kakapool	Periwinkle
(Allspice)	Jamaica Pepper	Queen of	
Old Maid	Periwinkle	Flowers	Pride of India
Palmiste	Cabbage Palm	Love Apple	Tomato
Primrose	Kew Plant	Manioc	Cassava
Old Man's		Belle Apple	Water Melon
Beard	Mistletoe	Barbadine	Granadilla
Flower Fence	Barbados Pride	Stinging Nettle	Scratch Bush
Bois Canot	Trumpet Tree	Lady of the	
Shaddock	Forbidden Fruit	Night	Tree of Sadness
Adlay	Job's Tears	Shame Plant	Sensitive Plant
Melongene	Egg Plant	Tee Marie	Sensitive Plant
Dasheen	Chinese Eddoes	Bois Flot	Cork Wood
Fat Pork	Cocoa Plum	Bodi	Yard Bean
Pomme Malac		Black Eye Pea	Cow Pea
(Pomerack)	Malacca Apple		

MISCELLANEOUS

The five Senses or gateways of knowledge are seeing, hearing, feeling, smelling and tasting.

The Four Elements (*Ancient*) are fire, water, air, earth.

The Dead Languages are Ancient Greek and Latin.

The Three Professions are Divinity, Law, Medicine.

The Lake Poets are Coleridge, Southey, Wordsworth.

The Latin Races are French, Spanish, Portuguese, Italians.

A Decade is a period of ten years.

A Generation—about thirty years.

A Century—one hundred years.

A Millennium—one thousand years.

Cardinal Numbers are 1, 2, 3, 4, 5 etc.

Ordinal Numbers are 1st, 2nd, 3rd, 4th, 5th etc.

Cardinal Points are North, South, East, West.

Cardinal Signs are Aries, Libra, Cancer, Capricorn.

Cardinal Virtues are (a) Prudence, Temperance, Justice, Fortitude, or (b) Faith, Hope, Charity.

All Fools' Day	—April 1st
All Saints' Day	—November 1st
All Souls' Day	—November 2nd
Ash Wednesday	—The first day of Lent
Valentine's Day	—February 14th

THE METRIC SYSTEM

Linear Measure

10 millimetres (mm)	= 1 centimetre (cm)
100 centimetres	= 1 metre (m)
1000 metres	= 1 kilometre (km)

Square Measure

100 square millimetres (mm²)	= 1 square centimetre (cm²)
10,000 square centimetres	= 1 square metre (m²)
1,000,000 square metres	= 1 square kilometre (km²)

Land Measure

1 square metre	= 1 centiare
100 centiares	= 1 are
100 ares	= 1 hectare (ha)
100 hectares	= 1 square kilometre

Fluid Measure

10 millilitres	= 1 centilitre
100 centilitres	= 1 litre

Temperature

Freezing point of water	= 0° Celsius (centigrade) (C) = 32° Fahrenheit (F)
Boiling point of water	= 100 °C = 212 °F
To convert Fahrenheit to Celsius	= (°F-32) × 5/9 = °C

Weight

1000 grams	= 1 kilogram (kg)
1000 kilograms	= 1 tonne

Capacity

1000 cubic centimetres (cm³)	= litre (l)
1000 litres	= 1 cubic metre (m³)

Approximate Metric Equivalents

1 inch	= 25·4 millimetres
1 yard	= 0·91 metres
1 fathom	= 1·83 metres
1 chain	= 20·12 metres
1 mile	= 1·61 kilometres
	= 1,610 metres
1 square yard	= 0·84 square metres
1 square mile	= 2·59 square kilometres
1 acre	= 0·4 hectares
1 fluid ounce	= 28 cubic centimetres
1 pint	= 0·57 litres
1 gallon	= 4·55 litres
1 gallon (U.S.)	= 3·79 litres
1 ounce	= 28 grammes
1 pound	= 0·45 kilogrammes
1 ton	= 1,016 kilogrammes
1 metric tonne	= 1,000 kilogrammes
	= 2,204 pounds
1 cubic yard	= 0·76 cubic metres
1 centimetre	= 0·39 inches
1 metre	= 3·28 feet
	= 1·09 yards
1 kilometre	= 0·62 miles
1 square metre	= 10·76 square feet
	= 1·2 square yards
1 hectare	= 2·47 acres
1 square kilometre	= 0·39 square miles
1 litre	= 1·76 pints
1 kilogramme	= 2·2 pounds

THE IMPERIAL SYSTEM

Linear Measure

1 yard	= 36 inches
1 furlong	= 220 yards
1 mile	= 8 furlongs
	= 1,760 yards
	= 5,280 feet
1 league	= 3 miles
1 chain	= 22 yards
	= 66 feet

Land Measure

144 sq. ins.	= 1 sq. ft.
9 sq. ft.	= 1 sq. yd.
484 sq. yds.	= 1 sq. chain
10 sq. chains	= 1 acre
1 acre	= 4,840 sq. yds.
	= 43,560 sq. ft.
640 acres	= 1 sq. mile

Measures of Capacity

| 1,728 cubic in. | = 1 cubic foot |
| 27 cubic feet | = 1 cubic yard |

Measures of Weight

16 ounces	= 1 pound
14 pounds	= 1 stone
28 pounds	= 1 quarter
4 quarters	= 1 cwt. (hundredw't)
112 pounds	= 1 cwt.
20 cwt.	= 1 ton
2,240 pounds	= 1 ton (long)

Fluid Measure

2 pints	= 1 quart
4 quarts	= 1 gallon
8 pints	= 1 gallon

Measures of Numbers

1 dozen	= 12 units
1 score	= 20 units
1 gross	= 144 units
1 quire	= 24 sheets of paper
1 ream	= 20 quires
1 bale	= 10 reams

Nautical or Graphical Measure

6 feet	= 1 fathom
120 fathoms	= 1 cable
6,080 feet	= 1 knot (nautical mile)

Roman Numerals

I =	1
V =	5
X =	10
L =	50
C =	100
D =	500
M =	1,000

When a character is followed by another of less or equal value, the number expressed denotes the sum of their single values, but when preceded by one of less value, it signifies the difference.

e.g.

III	=	3		
IV	=	4	VI =	6
XL	=	40	LX =	60
CD	=	400	DC =	600
MCMXLVI	=	1946		

Arabic Numerals consist of

0, 1, 2, 3, 4, 5, 6, 7, 8, 9, so called because they were introduced into Europe by the Arabs.

ARITHMETICAL FORMULAE

SQUARE: (a) Area of square = Side squared $= S^2$
(b) Perimeter of Square = Side $\times 4 = S \times 4$
(c) To find the side, Area being given:
Take the square root of the Area
$$\therefore S = \sqrt{A}$$

RHOMBUS: Area of Rhombus = base $\times$ perpendicular height
$$= B \times H$$

RECTANGLE:

(a) Area of Rectangle = Length $\times$ Breadth $= L \times B$

(b) Length of Rectangle = Area $\div$ Breadth $= \dfrac{A}{B}$

(c) Breadth of Rectangle = Area $\div$ Length $= \dfrac{A}{L}$

(d) Perimeter of Rectangle $= 2$ (length $+$ breadth) $= 2(L + B)$

PARALLELOGRAM:

Area of Parallelogram = base $\times$ perpendicular height $= B \times H$

TRIANGLE:

(a) Area of Triangle $= \frac{1}{2}$(base $\times$ perp. height)
$$= \tfrac{1}{2}(B \times H) \text{ or } \frac{B \times H}{2}$$

(b) Height of Triangle = (Area $\times 2$) $\div$ base $= \dfrac{A \times 2}{B}$

(c) Base of Triangle = (Area $\times 2$) $\div$ height $= \dfrac{A \times 2}{H}$

(d) To find the Area of a Triangle, the lengths of the three sides being given.

RULE: From half the sum of the three sides subtract each side

Arithmetical formulae (*contd.*)

separately; then find the continued product of the half and the three remainders; finally extract the square root of the product.

Thus Area $= \sqrt{s(s-a)(s-b)(s-c)}$

where s is used to denote half the sum of its sides, and a, b, c, the lengths of the three sides.

THE RIGHT-ANGLED TRIANGLE:

In any Right-Angled Triangle the square on the hypotenuse is equal to the sum of the squares on the other two sides.

(a) Hypotenuse $= \sqrt{\text{perp.}^2 + \text{base}^2} = \sqrt{p^2 + b^2}$

(b) Perpendicular $= \sqrt{\text{hypotenuse}^2 - \text{base}^2} = \sqrt{h^2 - b^2}$

(c) Base $= \sqrt{\text{hypotenuse}^2 - \text{perpendicular}^2}$

$\qquad = \sqrt{h^2 - p^2}$

TRAPEZIUM:

Area $= \frac{1}{2}$ width $\times$ (sum of parallel sides) $= \frac{1}{2} w(a+b)$

AREA OF THE FOUR WALLS OF A ROOM

Area of 4 walls = Twice the sum of the length and breadth of the room $\times$ height

$\qquad = 2(L+B) \times H$

SIMPLE INTEREST:

(a) Simple Interest $= \dfrac{\text{Principal} \times \text{Rate} \times \text{Time}}{100} = \dfrac{P \times R \times T}{100}$

(b) Principal $= \dfrac{\text{Interest} \times 100}{\text{Rate} \times \text{Time}} = \dfrac{I \times 100}{R \times T}$

(c) Rate $= \dfrac{\text{Interest} \times 100}{\text{Principal} \times \text{Time}} = \dfrac{I \times 100}{P \times T}$

Arithmetical formulae (contd.)

(d) Time $= \dfrac{\text{Interest} \times 100}{\text{Principal} \times \text{Rate}} = \dfrac{I \times 100}{P \times R}$

(e) Amount $= \text{Principal} + \text{Interest} = P + I$

CIRCLE:

(a) Circumference of Circle $= \text{diameter} \times \pi = d \times \pi$
  or $= \text{twice radius} \times \pi = 2\pi R$

(b) Diameter $\qquad = \text{Circumference} \div \pi = \dfrac{C}{\pi}$

(c) Radius $\qquad = \text{Circumference} \div 2\pi = \dfrac{C}{2\pi}$

(d) Area of Circle (when radius is given)
  $= \text{Radius squared multiplied by } \pi = \pi R^2$

(e) Area of Circle (when diameter is given)
  $= \text{one quarter of the diameter squared multiplied by } \pi$
  $= \dfrac{\pi D^2}{4}$

(f) Area of Circle (when circumference is given)
  (i) Divide the square of the Circumference by four times π
  $= \dfrac{C^2}{4\pi}$

or   (ii) Multiply the square of the Circumference by $\dfrac{7}{88}$

  $= C^2 \times \dfrac{7}{88}$

(g) To find the Radius, area being given
  Divide the area by π then extract the square root.

  $= \sqrt{\text{Area} \div \pi}$

(h) To find the Circumference, area being given
  (i) Multiply the area by four times π then extract the square root.
  $= \sqrt{\text{Area} \times 4\pi}$

Arithmetical formulae (*contd.*)

or (ii) Multiply the area by π, extract the square root, then multiply the results by two.

$$= 2\sqrt{\text{Area} \times \pi}$$

CIRCULAR RING:

To find the Area of a Circular Ring, multiply the product of the sum and difference of the inner and outer radii by π

$$= \pi(R+r)(R-r)$$

CYLINDER:

(a) To find the Area of Curved Surface of Cylinder, multiply the circumference of the cylinder by the height.
Area of Curved Surface $= 2\pi r \times h$

(b) Area of Total Surface of Cylinder
$=$ Area of Curved Surface $+$ Area of ends. $= 2\pi rh + 2\pi r^2$
or multiply the sum of the height and radius by the Circumference
$=$ Circumference $\times$ (height $+$ radius) $= c(h+r)$

(c) Volume of Cylinder $=$ Area of Base $\times$ height $= \pi r^2 h$

CONE:

(a) To find Curved Surface of Cone, multiply the product of radius and slant height by π
Curved Surface of Cone $= \pi rl$ (where l denotes slant height)

(b) Area of Total Surface of Cone
$=$ Area of Base $+$ Area of Curved Surface $= \pi r^2 + \pi rl$

(c) Volume of Cone $=$ Area of base $\times \frac{1}{3}$ perpendicular height.

$$= 2\pi r^2 \times \frac{h}{3}$$

THE SPHERE:

(a) Area of Surface of a Sphere $= 4\pi r^2$

(b) Volume of Sphere $\qquad = \dfrac{4\pi r^3}{3}$

Arithmetical formulae (*contd.*)

THE PRISM:

(1) Lateral surface of prism = (perimeter of base) × height.
(2) The Total surface of prism = lateral surface + area of ends.
(3) Volume of Prism = (area of base) × height.

THE PYRAMID:

(1) Area of Slant Surface of Pyramid
    = $\frac{1}{2}$ (perimeter of base) × slant height.
(2) Total Surface of Pyramid = slant surface + area of base.
(3) Volume of Pyramid = $\frac{1}{3}$ (area of base) × height.

RECTANGULAR SOLIDS:

(a) To find the Area of Surface of a Rectangular Solid, take the sum
    of the Areas of the six faces.
    ∴ Total Surface = $2(lb + bh + lh)$
    Where l denotes length; b breadth; h height.
(b) Volume of Rectangular Solid = length × breadth × height
    $$= l \times b \times h$$
    (i) Length of Rectangular Solid = Volume ÷ (base × height)
    $$= \frac{v}{b \times h}$$
    (ii) Breadth of Rectangular Solid = Volume ÷ (length × height)
    $$= \frac{v}{l \times h}$$
    (iii) Height of Rectangular Solid = Volume ÷ (length × breadth)
    $$= \frac{v}{l \times b}$$

THE CUBE:

(a) To find the Total Surface of a Cube, square the length of one side
    and multiply by 6.
    ∴ Total Surface = $2(a^2 + a^2 + a^2) = 6a^2$
(b) Volume of Cube = the cube of the length of the side
    $$= (a \times a \times a) = a^3$$

(c) To find the side of a cube, volume being given.
Take the cube root of the Volume
$$\therefore \text{Side} = \sqrt[3]{V}$$

DENSITY OR SPECIFIC GRAVITY:

(a) $\text{Density} = \dfrac{\text{Weight of Substance}}{\text{Weight of same Volume of Water}}$

(b) Weight of Substance = Density × weight of the same volume of water as the substance.

CIVICS

Civics has been defined as the science of citizenship and municipal government. The study of Civics in schools is intended to help children to become "upright and useful members of the community in which they live, and worthy sons and daughters of the country to which they belong."

THE FUNCTIONS OF GOVERNMENT

The main functions of Government are three in number:

(a) Legislative—the function of making, altering, amending or repealing laws. This is the work of the Legislature.

(b) Executive or Administrative—the work of putting the laws into effect, and of administering the country: these functions are performed by the Heads of Departments and other members of the Civil Service.

(c) Judicial—the function of explaining or interpreting the laws. This work is performed by the Law Courts which are presided over by Judges and Magistrates.

THE RIGHTS OF A CITIZEN

1. Perhaps the greatest privilege of a citizen is his right to share in the government of the country. He can do so directly if he becomes a member of the Legislative, Borough or County Council, or he can do so indirectly by exercising the franchise to elect suitable representatives to sit on the Councils.

2. In the eyes of the law all citizens are, broadly speaking, equal. Whatever our station in life, whether rich or poor, coloured or white, all of us are liable to punishment in the ordinary courts of law for breaches of the law.

186

3. Unless he has been suspected of committing a felony a policeman may not arrest a citizen without a warrant.
4. No citizen can be legally punished or deprived of his possessions except by the decisions of ordinary courts of law.
5. All citizens enjoy equal protection from the law. The protective hands of the Police Force are there for us all.
6. Every citizen enjoys personal freedom: short of breaking the law he is free to do what he likes. If a citizen is wrongfully deprived of his liberty he can obtain redress by recourse to the law courts.
7. Every citizen has a right to freedom of discussion. This means that he is free to say, write or publish anything he pleases so long as he does not commit a breach of the law.

   The law is infringed if he says or publishes anything of a defamatory, seditious, blasphemous, or obscene character.
8. Every citizen has the right to public meeting. People may meet together whenever or wherever they please in so far as they do not offend against the law. They can be apprehended for committing a nuisance, or trespass, or constituting an unlawful assembly. Also, the public have no right to meet in a public thoroughfare, or public resorts.
9. Every citizen enjoys the right of self-defence. He is justified in using a proportionate amount of force in defence of himself, his wife, his children, his house, or his property.

THE RESPONSIBILITIES OF A CITIZEN

1. A citizen's first duty is loyalty to his Ruler or Head of State, and country.
2. It is the duty of the citizen to obey all the laws of the land.
3. Since the revenue of Government is used to defray public expenditure, it is the duty of the citizen to pay all taxes and rates which he has to pay and not try to defraud the revenue.
4. If called upon to help, it is the duty of every citizen to give active aid to the Police in the apprehension of offenders.
5. The citizen must do all in his power to help to suppress a riot, or other outbursts of disorder, or to help repel an invasion.
6. It is his duty to aid the course of justice by giving evidence as a witness in criminal or police cases.
7. He has a responsibility to register the birth of his children soon

after they are born, to have them vaccinated, and to see that they receive elementary education.

The above are the legal statutory duties of a citizen, but it must not be supposed that the responsibilities of the citizen end with these. If a citizen faithfully adhered to the above he could be described as a law-abiding citizen. If he were apprised of all the information in the foregoing pages he might be considered an informed citizen. But these would not in themselves make him a good citizen.

It is important that the citizen should realize that he lives in a civilized society and that he has certain moral, social and community obligations.

In times like these there is no place for the "lone wolf." Our actions are dependent on the actions of others with whom we have to associate. If, therefore, we wish to be worthy citizens of our country, there are certain principles which we must try to observe. These are: (1) Proper human relationships; (2) Self-Independence; (3) Service to the community; (4) Observance of certain standards of conduct and behaviour.

1.   Proper human relationships or the art of living

This is an important element of good citizenship. This calls for (a) consideration for the feelings of others; (b) respect for the other persons' point of view; (c) co-operation.

(a) *Consideration for the feelings of others*

(i) So many of us want everything for ourselves and our families. Let us remember that other people have as much right to happiness and the good things of this world as we. We should all try to bear one another's burdens by acts of helpfulness when the need arises.

(ii) In the eyes of God all men are equal. Every person, regardless of his station in life has a dignity and importance far greater than the lower animals. He or she is a human being and should be treated as such.

(iii) All of us are proud of the things we do. Let us cultivate a sense of gratitude—the habit of giving due praise and thanks to people for what they do for us, or what they do for others because of us. Little gifts of flowers, Birthday or Christmas cards bring happiness both to the donor and the recipient. Also we must not be too ready to blame others, for we all make mistakes.

(iv) We must try to avoid the bullying, aggressive, scowling and critical attitude in our relations with our friends or subordinates.

(v) We must not be insubordinate to our superiors. Insubordination is distasteful to any employer. It antagonizes him and begets retaliation and victimization. In the long run it is the employee who suffers.

(vi) If we only have a thought to the untold misery which road accidents bring to the homes of so many families, we would all develop a better road sense and observe the Highway Code.

(b) *Respect for the other person's point of view*

This would be a dull and monotonous world if we all thought alike. It is said that variety is the spice of life. None of us has a monopoly of brains or ideas. We must therefore learn to be tolerant of the views and opinions of others. Don't do all the talking. Listen to what the other persons have to say even if their view on a question is not the same as yours. There may be a lot in what they have to say.

(c) *Co-operation*

It requires little thought to realize that we have to depend on each other at every turn of our lives. Production under the modern system is based on "division of labour" or "specialization," whereby several kinds of workers have to co-operate to turn out one finished manufactured article. Similarly no one today could be entirely self-sufficient in every respect. Every person has to depend on the labour of other people for certain commodities which he cannot produce himself. Thus all workers are dependent on others, whether they be agricultural, manual, factory, technical, clerical, administrative or professional workers.

2. Self-independence

It is the duty of the citizen while he has youth, strength and vigour to endeavour to make adequate preparation for himself and his family, so that neither he nor they will become a burden or charge on the community. The best ways to make this preparation are by:

(a) Being Thrifty: Save all you possibly can. Don't be extravagant in food, dress, or otherwise.

(b) Growing more food.
(c) Self Help: There are many worth-while organizations through which one may help oneself, *e.g.* Friendly Societies, Credit Unions and Co-operative Societies, Trade Unions.

3. Service to the community

This is one of the noblest duties of the citizen. A number of voluntary organizations such as the Red Cross Society, Child Welfare League, Boy Scout Movement, Girl Guide Movement, Village Councils, Literary and Cultural Clubs etc. offer innumerable opportunities for people to render service to the community. Incidentally, these organizations help to develop in their members the qualities of leadership and a sense of responsibility, just the type of citizen our country needs at the present time.

4. Observance of certain accepted standards of conduct and behaviour

These are legion, but mention is made only of those which are considered most important.
(a) Good citizens must come from good homes. The love of parents for their children and the affectionate regard of children for their parents are the first marks of a good home. Love, patience, and understanding should exist not only between father and mother but should embrace the entire family.
(b) Belief in religion: Every religion provides a code of rules to guide its members and to instil in them a sense of right and wrong.
(c) We owe it to Society to refrain from anything vulgar, indecent or immoral as regards our conduct and manner of dress.

Some don'ts for the young citizen

1. Don't do anything in public which will cause embarrassment or unpleasantness to others. For example, don't spit on the pavement,

don't shove your way to the front of a line if you are required to take your place in a queue, don't make uncomplimentary remarks about people as they pass along the street.

2. When speaking to other people—
   (a) Don't puff the smoke from your cigarette in their faces.
   (b) Don't monopolize the conversation. Give the other person a chance to say something also.
   (c) Don't argue about religion. It ends nowhere and usually leaves a lot of bitterness behind.

4. At parties or other social entertainments—
   (a) Don't take more than a just share. Leave some for the others.
   (b) Don't sponge. Bear your part of the expenses.

Chief human wants

The primary human wants are:
   (a) Air to breathe.
   (b) Water to drink and for trade and domestic purposes.
   (c) Adequate, wholesome and nourishing food.
   (d) Sufficient clothing to keep us warm and to enable us to conform to the accepted standards of decency.
   (e) Land on which to build our houses.
   (f) A house or shelter to protect us from the sun, wind and rain, and to ensure the privacy necessary for human beings in a civilized society.
   (g) A fire or fuel to enable us to cook our food.

THE COMMONWEALTH OF NATIONS

The Commonwealth of Nations, which has evolved from the British Empire is the largest voluntary association of nations the world has ever seen. It consists of:

The United Kingdom, which comprises England, Wales, Scotland, Northern Ireland, the Channel Islands and the Isle of Man; Canada; Australia; New Zealand; Jamaica; Grenada; Malaysia; Malta; Lesotho; Barbados; Mauritius; Swaziland; Tonga; Fiji; Western Samoa; Dominica; India; Sri Lanka; Ghana; Nigeria; Cyprus; Sierra Leone; Uganda; Kenya; Tanzania; Malawi; Zambia; The Gambia; Singapore; Guyana; Botswana; Nauru; Bangladesh; Trinidad and Tobago; Belize; Bahamas; Tuvalu; Papua New Guinea; St Lucia; St Vincent and the Grenadines; Solomon Islands; Kiribati; Vanuata; Zimbabwe and the Seychelles.

All of these territories enjoy full self-government and an equal status in all aspects of their democratic and external affairs. They are united by voluntary association with the Commonwealth, in which the United Kingdom is an equal member. They recognize the Queen as head of the Commonwealth although Republics do not accept her as their own sovereign.

The West Indies

The West Indies are a group of islands in the western hemisphere stretching in a curve from North America to South America and enclosing the Caribbean Sea. The whole group is within the Tropics. Neither The Bahamas nor Bermuda are part of the West Indies. Belize is part of Central America while Guyana is on the continent of South America.

Areas and Populations

	Area (km²)	Estimated Population	Capital	Capital's Population
Antigua	280 ⎫	74 000	St John's	24 000
Barbuda and Redonda	162 ⎭			
Barbados	429	246 100	Bridgetown	17 600
Dominica	751	74 100	Roseau	16 800
Grenada	344	110 400	St George's	10 000
Jamaica	11 424	2 190 000	Kingston	643 800
Turks and Caicos	430	7400		
Cayman Islands	259	17 000	Georgetown	7600
Montserrat	101	13 200	Plymouth	3500
St Kitts	174 ⎫	44 404	Basseterre	14 700
Nevis	130 ⎭			
Anguilla	88	6500		
St Lucia	616	140 000	Castries	51 240
St Vincent	389	120 000	Kingstown	23 221
Trinidad	4828	1 195 936	Port of Spain	59 437
Tobago	300	45 176		
	Adjacent Territories			
Guyana	214 970	865 000	Georgetown	183 000
Belize	22 962	144 800	Belmopan	2900
The Bahamas	11 406	209 500	Nassau	130 000
Bermuda	54	54 700	Hamilton	3000

WHAT FEDERATION MEANS

When a number of states or territories which were hitherto independent of one another desire to be under a single government for certain specific purposes they enter into a contract or treaty known as a Federation.

The form of the Federation is invariably set out in a written Constitution which provides for a Federal Government as distinct from the Unitary Governments which compose the Federation.

WEST INDIAN FEDERATION

The British West Indian Federation was a plant of slow and tender growth. As early as 1921, Major Wood, who afterwards became Lord Halifax, was sent out to the West Indies to investigate the possibility of establishing a Federation, but the idea was not pursued, because of the isolated nature of the territories due to lack of proper facilities for travel and inter-communication.

The idea was again pursued in 1945, but it was not until April 1958 that the West Indian Federation came into being.

Breakup of the Federation

The Federation did not last long because it was a *political* union of a number of islands with different levels of political advancement, and conflicts soon began to develop.

On 19 September, 1961, a Referendum was held in Jamaica and the electors voted in favour of Jamaica seceding from the Federation. The ruling Party in the Government of Trinidad and Tobago followed with a declaration that it would not participate in the Federation without Jamaica. As a consequence of these two withdrawals the United Kingdom Parliament passed The West Indies Act, 1962, on 3 April, 1962, which dissolved the West Indies Federation.

The federal idea is by no means dead, however, for many prominent West Indians are convinced that the salvation of the West Indies lies in a federation. Be that as it may, the failure of the last Federation is still fresh in the minds of West Indians for another experiment at political federation and most politicians are now thinking in terms of regional economic co-operation.

Towards a Caribbean Economic Community

The first major step towards this goal was taken on the initiative of the Prime Minister of Trinidad and Tobago. On the breakup of the Federation, the Government of Trinidad and Tobago had put forward a proposal for the establishment of a Caribbean Economic Community. In furtherance of this proposal, Heads of Government conferences were held in 1963, 1964 and 1967, when it was agreed by the Heads of Government to formally establish CARIFTA as the first step in the ultimate creation of a viable economic community of Caribbean Territories.

The new CARIFTA Agreement came into effect on 1 May, 1968, with the participation of Antigua, Barbados, Guyana and Trinidad and Tobago.

Dominica, Grenada, St Kitts-Nevis-Anguilla, St Lucia and St Vincent joined on 1 July, 1968; Jamaica and Montserrat were admitted on 1 August, 1968. while Belize became a member in May 1971. The Bahamas did not joint CARIFTA but was an active participant in other areas of regional co-operation.

Significant developments since CARIFTA

a) The establishment of the Commonwealth Caribbean Regional Secretariat on 1 May 1968 in Georgetown, Guyana, to administer the operations of CARIFTA (now known as the Caribbean Common Market).

b) The establishment of the Caribbean Development Bank in Barbados in October 1969 to provide funds for development, particularly for the benefit of the Less Developed Countries which receive preferential treatment as far as "soft loans" are concerned.

By Article 3 of the Treaty establishing the Caribbean Community the following countries have been designated as "Less Developed Countries (LDC's)": Antigua, Belize, Dominica, Grenada, Montserrat, St Kitts-Nevis-Anguilla, St Lucia and St Vincent. On the other hand, Barbados, Guyana, Jamaica, Trinidad and Tobago have been designated as "More Developed Countries (MDC's)."

c) An increase in the pace towards providing Common Services. In addition to the University of the West Indies, the West Indies Shipping Services and the Caribbean Meteorological Service which were continued after the breakup of the Federation a number of new institutions were set up for Common Services in the fields of health, technical assistance, legal education and Caribbean controlled examinations.

d) The decision to transform CARIFTA into a Common Market and to establish the Caribbean Community; the Common Market being part and parcel of the Caribbean Community. This decision was taken at the seventh Heads of Government Conference held at Chaguaramas, Trinidad, in October 1972.

e) The Georgetown Accord which was signed at the eighth Heads of Government Conference in April 1973 in Georgetown, Guyana, by all the members of CARIFTA with the exception of Antigua and Montserrat.

The Georgetown Accord provided for the coming into force on 1 June 1973 of three agreements, viz. (a) The harmonisation of fiscal incentives to industry; (b) The avoidance of double taxation; and (c) The establishment of the Caribbean Investment Corporation.

The Accord also provided for the signature of the Caribbean Community Treaty on 4 July 1973 and its coming into effect on 1 August 1973 among the four independent countries: Barbados, Guyana, Jamaica and Trinidad and Tobago. This was accomplished as planned.

On 17 April 1974 the following territories signed the CARICOM Treaty and were admitted to full membership in the Caribbean Community as had also been provided for in the Georgetown Accord: Grenada, St Vincent, St Lucia, The Bahamas, Montserrat, Dominica and Belize. The signing ceremony took place in Castries, St Lucia. Antigua was not represented and Mr Bradshaw refused to sign because the British Government had indicated that they would not agree to the inclusion of Anguilla as part of the state of St Kitts-Nevis.

Salient features of the CARICOM Treaty

1. The Caribbean Community will have three areas of activity, namely,
   (a) Economic integration through the Common Market;
   (b) Common Services and functional co-operation; and
   (c) The co-ordination of Foreign Policy among the independent countries.

2. The principal organs of the Community are the Heads of Government Conference and the Common Market Council. There are also a number of other bodies referred to as "Institutions".

   The Heads of Government Conference is comprised of the Heads of Government of the member states (the Prime Ministers, Premiers and Chief Minister). It is the highest policy-making body of the Community and may issue directions as to the policy to be pursued by the Common Market Council and other institutions of the Community. The Conference is the final authority for the conclusion of treaties on behalf of the Community and for entering into relationships between the Community and other international organisations and states.

The Common Market Council is the second most important organ in the Community. It is the successor to the CARIFTA Council and is directly responsible for the running of the Common Market.

The "Institutions" consist of the Conference of Ministers responsible for Health and six Standing Committees of Ministers responsible respectively for Education, Labour, Foreign Affairs, Finance, Agriculture and Mines. The Institutions may formulate such policies and perform such functions as are necessary for the achievement of the objectives of the Community.

(Further information on the Community and the Common Market can be obtained from an excellent handbook "The Caribbean Community—A Guide" published by the Caribbean Community Secretariat and available at bookstores.

THE CONSTITUTIONAL DEVELOPMENT OF JAMAICA, TRINIDAD AND TOBAGO, BARBADOS, THE WINDWARD AND LEEWARD ISLANDS, GUYANA, AND BELIZE

Jamaica

Jamaica was wrested from Spain for Britain by Admiral Penn and General Venables in 1655.

The island was granted a Constitution by King Charles II in 1662, which, with the exception of an amendment in 1854, lasted for over two hundred years. The original constitution consisted of a Governor, a Nominated Council, and an Elected Assembly of about 30 members. In 1854 a separated Privy Council was set up, and an Executive Council was established, mainly to deal with financial matters.

Following the 1865 unrest a Legislative Council was created in 1869 with 6 Official members and 6 Unofficial members appointed by Her Majesty. In 1878 the number of Official and Unofficial members was increased to 8, and in 1881 to 9 each.

With the coming into full effect of the Jamaica (Constitution) Order-in-Council, 1959, on 4 July, 1959, the island achieved complete internal self-government within the framework of the West Indies Federation. The principal changes brought about were: (i) The Executive Council was replaced by the Cabinet. (ii) The Chief Minister was re-named Premier. (iii) The House of Representatives was increased from 32 to 45 members.

On 19 September, 1961, a Referendum was held in Jamaica and the electors voted in favour of Jamaica seceding from The West Indies Federation. Following this development Jamaica began talks with the British Government for Jamaica to achieve its independence as a separate nation. The Party then in power (Mr Manley's P.N.P.) and the Opposition (J.L.P.) having agreed on a constitution acceptable to the Secretary of State for the Colonies, Jamaica attained the status of an independent nation within the British Commonwealth of Nations on 6 August, 1962.

The following are the main provisions of the Independence Constitution.

Parliament

The Parliament of Jamaica consists of Her Majesty, a Senate and a House of Representatives. Its main function is to make laws for the peace, order and good government of Jamaica.

Governor-General

The Governor-General of Jamaica is appointed by Her Majesty and will hold office during Her Majesty's pleasure. He will be Her Majesty's representative in Jamaica.

The Senate

The Senate consists of 21 Senators of whom:

(a) 13 Senators are appointed by the Governor-General acting in accordance with the advice of the Prime Minister.

(b) 8 Senators are appointed by the Governor-General acting in accordance with the advice of the Leader of the Opposition.

The Senate will be presided over by a President or a Deputy President elected from among the Senators who are not Ministers or Parliamentary Secretaries at the first meeting of the Senate after any dissolution of Parliament.

A quorum of the Senate shall consist of 8 members besides the person presiding.

The House of Representatives

The House of Representatives consists of 60 members as provided by Order of the Governor-General acting on the recommendation of the Standing Committee of the House of Representatives. For the purpose of election of members to the House of Representatives, Jamaica shall be divided into not less than 60 constituencies, one member being returned for each constituency.

The Speaker and the Deputy Speaker of the House of Representatives shall be elected from among the members of that House who are not Ministers or Parliamentary Secretaries when the House of Representatives first meets after any dissolution of Parliament.

Voting

A quorum of the House of Representatives shall consist of 16 members besides the person presiding.

Except as otherwise provided in the Constitution, all questions proposed for decision in either House are determined by a majority of the votes of the members present and voting.

The person presiding in either House shall not vote unless on any question the votes are equally divided, in which case, he shall have and exercise a casting vote; or except in the case of a final vote on a Bill for special Acts of Parliament relating to either the lowering of the prescribed age for the qualification of electors from 21 years to not less than 18 years, or to alteration of the Constitution, in each of which cases he shall have an original vote.

Money and other Bills

A Money Bill shall not be introduced in the Senate. A Bill other than a Money Bill may be introduced in either House.

The Senate has no power to delay a Money Bill passed by the House of Representatives for longer than one month. With regard to a Bill other than a Money Bill the Senate's power to delay this is restricted to rejection by the Senate twice in the same session, provided seven months have elapsed between the first and second sessions, or in two successive sessions provided six months have elapsed between the sessions after which, unless the House of Representatives otherwise resolves, the Governor-General will give his assent notwithstanding that the Senate has not consented to the Bill.

The Executive

The Executive Authority of Jamaica is vested in Her Majesty and may be exercised on Her Majesty's behalf by the Governor-General, either directly or through officers subordinate to him.

The Cabinet

The Cabinet of Jamaica shall consist of the Prime Minister and such number of other Ministers (not being less than 11), selected from among Ministers appointed in accordance with the provisions of Section 70 of this Constitution, as the Prime Minister may from time to time consider appropriate.

The Cabinet is the principal instrument of policy and is charged with the general direction and control of the Government of Jamaica and is collectively responsible therefore to Parliament.

Whenever the Governor-General has occasion to appoint a Prime Minister he appoints the member of the House of Representatives who, in his judgment, is best able to command the confidence of the majority of the members of that House.

Not less than 2 nor more than 4 of the Ministers shall be persons who are members of the Senate.

The Prime Minister shall, so far as practicable, attend and preside at all meetings of the Cabinet. He shall keep the Governor-General fully informed concerning the general conduct of the Government of Jamaica and shall furnish the Governor-General with such information as he may request with respect to any particular matter relating to the Government of Jamaica.

The Governor-General, acting on the advice of the Prime Minister may appoint Parliamentary Secretaries from among the members of the two Houses to assist Ministers in the discharge of their functions.

The Governor-General shall appoint as Leader of the Opposition the member of the House of Representatives who in his judgment is best able to command the support of the majority of those members who do not support the Government.

Privy Council and Service Commissions

The Constitution also makes provision for a Privy Council, a Judicial Service Commission, a Public Service Commission and a Police Service Commission.

Trinidad and Tobago

Trinidad was discovered by Christopher Columbus on his third voyage on 31 July, 1498. Columbus took possession of the island in the name of Spain, but it was not until 1532 that the King of Spain appointed a Governor to rule the colony. The Spanish form of Government was introduced and in 1592 St Joseph was founded and declared the capital.

In 1797, England being then at war with Spain, Sir Ralph Abercromby captured Trinidad for the British, and Lieutenant-Colonel Picton became Trinidad's first British Governor.

At the time of the capitulation the Spanish type of Crown Colony Government had been firmly established in the colony. Assisting the Governor was a council called the Cabildo, "a body corporate that partook of the mixed nature of an ecclesiastical council, a parish vestry, a municipal corporation, and a council of government." In order to avoid confusion amongst the population the British Government did not decide on any sudden change in the Constitution but carried on the Spanish form of Government, including Spanish Law, with the advice of the Cabildo. The English system of Government was only gradually introduced while the powers of the Cabildo were progressively reduced. In 1841 the Cabildo was converted into the Town Council of Port-of-Spain and Spanish law was repealed entirely in 1845.

In 1801 the British Governor Picton appointed a **Council of Advice** consisting of five influential members of the community to assist him in managing the country. This later became His Majesty's Council.

By the year 1813 it had become firmly established that the predominant racial elements should be represented on the Council and it became customary for a Spaniard, a Frenchman, and an Englishman to be nominated.

The next constitutional change took place in 1831 with the creation of a **Legislative Council** of 12 members, 6 Official members and 6 other members nominated by the Governor from among the big proprietors of the colony. An **Executive Council** was also formed consisting of the members of His Majesty's Council.

Tobago was annexed in 1889 and for the purpose of administration it was united with Trinidad under one Government, in 1898.

The year 1924 witnessed a big Constitutional advance when the elected element was introduced in the Legislature for the first time.

In 1941 there was a further constitutional advance. By an increase in the elected element and a reduction of the official element, the number of elected members was made equal to the Nominated Unofficial and Official members combined.

The Legislative Council of 1941 consisted of 18 members: 9 Elected members, 6 Nominated Unofficial members and 3 Official members.

In 1945 universal adult suffrage was granted to the colony, and the qualifications for Elected members were reduced.

Further constitutional advances

Further constitutional changes took place in 1950 and 1956 resulting in the creation of the Office of Chief Minister, an increase in the number of elected members and also of other ministers.

On 3 July, 1959, Trinidad and Tobago achieved a greater measure of self-government with the introduction of Cabinet Government.

Full internal self-government

Following constitutional discussions held in London and Trinidad a new constitution was established for Trinidad and Tobago on 26 June, 1961. The provisions became effective on Tuesday, 19 December, and marked the coming into force of full internal self-government for the territory.

The 4 December election resulted in a victory for the People's National Movement whose party won 20 of the 30 seats contested, the other 10 going to the Democratic Labour Party.

Independence

As a result of constitutional talks held in London in May, 1962, Trinidad and Tobago became an independent nation on 31 August, 1962.

The first General Election after Independence was held on 7 November, 1966. The People's National Movement won 24 seats and the Democratic Labour Party, 12. In the 1971 General Election, the People's National Movement won all 36 seats. The Democratic Labour Party did not contest the Elections. In the 1976 election, the People's National Movement won 27 seats.

The Republic of Trinidad and Tobago

An Act to establish the Republic of Trinidad and Tobago and to enact a new Constitution in place of the former Constitution was passed by the appropriate number of votes in the House of Representatives and also the Senate, and was assented to on 29 March, 1976. The main features of the Constitution are:

The Republic of Trinidad and Tobago is a sovereign democratic State.

Fundamental human rights and freedoms are enshrined in the Constitution.

There shall be a President of Trinidad and Tobago who shall be Head of State and Commander-in-Chief of the armed forces. He shall be elected by the Electoral College consisting of all the members of the Senate and all the members of the House of Representatives assembled together as a unicameral body. The President shall normally hold office for five years. The President of the Senate shall act temporarily for the President if the office of President becomes vacant or if the President is incapable of performing his functions as President by reason of his absence from Trinidad and Tobago or by reason of illness.

Parliament

There shall be a Parliament of Trinidad and Tobago which shall consist of the President, the Senate and the House of Representatives.

The Senate shall consist of 31 Senators, of whom:

(a) 16 shall be appointed by the President acting in accordance with the advice of the Prime Minister.

(b) 6 shall be appointed by the President acting in accordance with the advice of the Leader of the Opposition; and

(c) 9 shall be appointed by the President in his discretion from outstanding persons from economic or social or community organizations and other major fields of endeavour.

The Senate will be presided over by a President elected from among the Senators. A Vice-President will also be elected from among the Senators.

The President of the Senate or other member presiding in the Senate shall not vote unless on any question the votes are equally divided, in which case he shall have and exercise a casting vote.

A quorum of the Senate shall consist of 10 Senators not including the person presiding at the sitting of the Senate.

The House of Representatives shall consist of 36 Elected members or such other number of members as corresponds with the number of constituencies into which Trinidad and Tobago is divided. The election of members of the House of Representatives shall be by secret ballot and in accordance with the first-past-the-post system.

The House of Representatives elects a person to be Speaker of the House. The Speaker may be elected either from among the members of the House of Representatives who are not Ministers or Parliamentary Secretaries, or from among persons who are not members of either House. A Deputy Speaker shall also be elected from among the members of the House who are not Ministers or Parliamentary Secretaries.

The Speaker or, in his absence, the Deputy Speaker, shall preside at each sitting of the House of Representatives.

The Speaker or other Member presiding in the House of Representatives shall not vote unless on any question the votes are equally divided, in which case he shall have and exercise a casting vote.

A quorum of the House of Representatives shall consist of twelve members of the House, not including the person presiding at that sitting of the House.

Money and other Bills

The power of Parliament to make laws, except where otherwise authorized by Statute, shall be exercised by Bills passed by the House of

Representatives and the Senate and assented to by the President.

A Money Bill shall not be introduced in the Senate. A Bill other than a Money Bill may be introduced in either House.

The Senate has no power to delay a Money Bill passed by the House of Representatives for longer than one month.

Where a Bill other than a Money Bill having been passed by the House of Representatives in two successive sessions, and having been sent to the Senate in each of those sessions one month before the end of the session, is rejected by the Senate in each of those sessions, then that Bill could be presented to the President for assent notwithstanding that the Senate has not consented to the Bill. The only proviso is that at least six months should have elapsed between the date on which the Bill is passed by the House of Representatives in the first session and the date on which the identical Bill or substantially the same Bill is passed by the House of Representatives in the second session.

The President, acting in accordance with the advice of the Prime Minister, may at any time prorogue or dissolve Parliament.

Parliament, unless sooner dissolved, shall continue for five years from the date of its first sitting after any dissolution, and shall then stand dissolved; except that at any time when Trinidad and Tobago is at war, the life of Parliament may be extended beyond the period of five years, for not more than twelve months at a time up to a maximum extension of five years.

Executive powers

The executive authority of Trinidad and Tobago shall be vested in the President and, subject to the Constitution, may be exercised by him either directly or through officers subordinate to him.

The Cabinet

There shall be a Cabinet for Trinidad and Tobago which shall have the general direction and control of the government of Trinidad and Tobago and shall be collectively responsible therefore to Parliament. The Cabinet shall consist of the Prime Minister and such number of other Ministers (of whom one shall be the Attorney General) as the Prime Minister may consider appropriate.

The President shall appoint as **Prime Minister** a member of the House of Representatives who is the Leader in that House of the party which commands the support of the majority of members of that House. However, if it appears to the President that no party commands the support of a majority of members he shall appoint the member of the House of Representatives who, in his judgment, is most likely to command the support of the majority of members of that House and who is willing to accept the office.

The **Ministers** other than the Prime Minister shall be such persons as the President, acting in accordance with the advice of the Prime Minister, shall appoint from among the members of the House of Representatives and the Senators.

In this exercise of his functions the President shall act in accordance with the advice of the Cabinet or a Minister acting under the general authority of the Cabinet, except in cases where provision is made under the Constitution or any other law for him to act otherwise.

The Prime Minister shall keep the President fully informed concerning the general conduct of the government of Trinidad and Tobago and shall furnish the President with such information as he may request with respect to any particular matter relating to the government of Trinidad and Tobago.

There shall be an office of Leader of the Opposition. The President shall, if the person is willing to be appointed, appoint as Leader of the Opposition the member of the House of Representatives who, in his judgment, is best able to command the support of the greatest number of members of the House of Representatives who do not support the Government.

Tobago, like Trinidad, was discovered by Columbus in 1498. It remained uninhabited for many years. In 1632 it was occupied by a number of Zealanders. During the Seven Years' War Admiral Rodney and General Monckton captured Tobago for the British. The island changed hands, however, during the American War of Independence when it was captured by the French. In 1803, during the Napoleonic War, Britain again took possession of Tobago when Commodore Hood and General Grinfield captured it, and at the peace of 1814 it was formally ceded to Britain.

The Constitution of Tobago in 1814 was very advanced. It consisted of a Bi-Cameral Legislature—the House of Assembly, and the Legislative Council—a Privy Council, and Law Courts similar to those in England.

As a result of severe economic depression following upon the decline of the sugar industry in the West Indies, Tobago along with other West Indian Islands, voluntarily relinquished a lot of its constitutional freedom and accepted Crown Colony Government. In 1874 its House of Assembly was abolished and a single chamber Legislative Council was formed, and in 1877 after the Belmanna riots Tobago became a Crown Colony on the request of its Legislative Council.

Further economic depression as a result of a fall in the price of sugar, and the failure of the "Metayer" system of cane farming caused the island to be annexed to Trinidad as a joint Colony on the 1 January, 1889. Less than ten years later, the economic position having deteriorated still further, the island was made a ward of the Colony of Trinidad and Tobago, in October, 1898. In 1980 Tobago was granted internal autonomy with the establishment of the Tobago House of Assembly.

Barbados

Unlike most of the other West Indian Islands, Barbados was not discovered by Columbus.

Towards the end of 1624, or early in 1625, a ship belonging to Sir William Courteen and captained by John Powell touched at the island. Some of the crew landed and claimed the island in the name of King James of England. Following this, in 1623, Sir William Courteen sent out to the island 40 settlers in the ship *William and John*, under the command of Captain Henry Powell, the younger brother of Captain John Powell. The settlers built a fort which they named Plantation Fort and founded the town of Jamestown or Hole Town, with Captain Deane as their Governor. New settlers from England swelled the number of colonists, and it is estimated that by 1628, the little colony had a population of about 2,000 settlers.

Meanwhile, in 1627, King Charles I had made a grant of all the Caribbean islands to the Earl of Carlisle. Under this grant the Earl sent settlers to Barbados who landed in Carlisle Bay and established Bridgetown, with Wolferstone as their Governor.

A year later, under the mistaken impression that Barbados was not one of the Caribbean islands, King Charles I granted the island to the Earl of Pembroke. On discovering that the Earl of Carlisle had already been granted possession of Barbados, the Earl of Pembroke allied himself with Sir William Courteen's Colony at Hole Town and supported their claim for possession of the island on the grounds of pre-occupation. Conflict ensued between the Leeward (Hole Town) and Windward (Bridgetown) settlers until the former were overpowered by Lord Carlisle's settlers.

Lord Carlisle died in 1636, and his son leased the island for 21 years to Lord Willoughby of Parham, who assumed the governorship of the island. During the Civil War Lord Willoughby ranged himself on the side of the Royalists, and, as an enemy of the Commonwealth, he was forced to capitulate to the Cromwellian fleet in 1652. The Commonwealth Government replaced Lord Willoughby by another Governor. After the Restoration the claims of Lord Carlisle's Patent were renewed, but an agreement was made to surrender the Patent to the Crown in return for a compensation of $4\frac{1}{2}\%$ of duty on exports. Although the duty continued to be payable until 1838, proprietary rule came to an end in 1652.

Barbados has always had some form of representative institution. It has the second oldest Parliament in the Commonwealth, the legislature being formed in 1639. The creation of an Executive Committee in 1881 was the first step towards the Ministerial government in 1954.

Barbados remained a British possession from early settlement until 1966 when it became a Sovereign State and a member of the Commonwealth.

The Legislature

The present legislature consists of the Governor-General who represents Her Majesty and is appointed by her, a Senate and a House of Assembly.

The Senate comprises 21 members appointed by the Governor-General, 12 of whom are appointed on the advice of the Prime Minister, 2 on the advice of the Leader of the Opposition and 7 appointed to represent the religious, economic or social interest in the island or such other interests as the Governor-General considers ought to be represented.

The House of Assembly consists of 24 members elected on the basis of Universal Adult Suffrage, the qualifying age being 18 years. The House has a normal life of 5 years.

Executive Government

The executive authority is Her Majesty and is exercised on her behalf by the Governor-General. He is advised by the Cabinet or a Minister acting under the general authority of the Cabinet. The general government and control of legislation rests with the Cabinet.

The Cabinet consists of the Prime Minister and at least 5 other members, the exact number being determined by the Governor-General. The Governor-General also controls appointment in the public service, but in all other matters he acts in accordance with the advice of an Executive Committee.

In 1954 a Ministerial System was introduced and a Premier was appointed. On 30 November, 1966, Barbados attained the status of an independent Sovereign state, and has elected to remain as a member of the Commonwealth of Nations. Previous to independence General Elections were held on 3 November, and the ruling Democratic Labour Party won 14 of the 24 seats in the House of Assembly: the Barbados Labour Party won 8 and the Barbados National Party won 2. By 1981, the number of seats had risen to 27, of which the Barbados Labour Party won 17 and the Democratic Labour Party 10.

The Windward and Leeward Islands

Up to the end of 1959 the Windward Islands—Grenada, St Lucia, St Vincent and Dominica—were grouped for purposes of administration under the Governor of the Windward Islands. The Leeward Islands—Antigua, St Kitts (including Nevis and Anguilla), and Montserrat—were grouped under the Governor of the Leeward Islands.

As from 1 January, 1960, each of the above-named islands was granted a new constitution which provided for it to be administered as a separate territory. Each territory had an Administrator, an Executive Council, and a Legislative Council.

The most recent constitutional development for the Windward and Leeward Islands (which became effective in 1967) was a non-colonial relationship between Britain and Grenada, St Vincent, St Lucia, Dominica, Antigua and St Kitts-Nevis-Anguilla. This relationship established a free and voluntary association between Britain and each of these islands, terminable by either country at any time. The new association provided for a new constitution under which each island would be fully self-governing in all its internal affairs; Britain's would be responsible for defence and external relations but the arrangements with regard to these provided the fullest possible consultation, operated in a spirit of co-operation and mutual confidence. The islands continued to be eligible to receive aid from Britain.

Grenada: On 15 August, 1498, on his third voyage, Christopher Columbus discovered Grenada, which he called Conception.

One of the earliest attempts at settlement was in 1609 by a Company of London Merchants. This was short lived because the settlers were unable to withstand the constant harassing from the hostile natives, the Caribs. Later, a French Trading Company made settlements on the island. The company sold the island, in 1650, to Du Parquet, the Governor of Martinique, who established a settlement at St George's. This settlement did not prove a financial success and Du Parquet sold to the Comte de Cerillac. In 1665 Colbert, the French Finance Minister, purchased a number of West Indian islands for the French Crown, among them being Grenada, and placed them under the control of the French West India Company. Maladministration and corruption, however, made it necessary for the French Crown to assume direct control. This was done in 1674.

During the Seven Years' War between Britain and France, Grenada was conquered by the British under Commodore Swanton, in 1762, and was formally ceded to Britain by the Treaty of Paris, 1763. It was recaptured for the French by Comte d'Estaing in 1779 during the War of American Independence, but was restored to Britain by the Treaty of Versailles, 1783. Since that time it remained in the possession of the British until Grenada became an Independent State within the Commonwealth on 7 February, 1974.

In 1978 Prime Minister Eric Gairy was overthrown and a new Revolutionary People's Government led by Maurice Bishop took over, although Commonwealth ties were retained. Maurice Bishop was killed in 1983 by dissidents within his own party.

St Vincent was discovered by Columbus in 1498. The island was then inhabited by Caribs and these remained undisturbed until 1627 when King Charles I granted a patent to the Earl of Carlisle for all the Caribbean Islands, among them being St Vincent. In 1660 England and France agreed that St Vincent should remain neutral as a home for the Caribs, but in spite of this agreement, King Charles II granted the island to Lord Willoughby in 1672. About this time a number of

African slaves who were shipwrecked in the Grenadines managed to reach St Vincent where they made settlements and intermarried with the Caribs. French settlements were also made along the Leeward coast and in Kingstown. By the treaty of Aix-la-Chapelle in 1748, St Vincent was again declared neutral, but in 1762 it was captured by the British who took possession of it, and after the peace of 1763, introduced European settlers. During the War of American Independence, St Vincent was captured by the French but it was restored to England at the Treaty of Versailles in 1783. It remained in the possession of Britain until 1979 when St Vincent became fully independent as a member of the Commonwealth.

St Lucia was discovered by Columbus on his fourth voyage in June, 1502. At that time the island was inhabited by the Caribs and it remained in their possession until 1635 when the King of France granted it to MM de L'Olive and Duplessis. In 1639 the first English settlers arrived in the island but in the following year they were all murdered by the Caribs.

In 1642 the French King, still claiming sovereignty over the island, granted it to the French West India Company, who in 1650 sold it to MM Honel and Du Parquet. As a result of a treaty with the Caribs, St Lucia agreed to take the surplus population of Barbados and in 1664 Lord Willoughby sent an expedition of 1000 Barbadians to the island. The Barbadians easily overcame the French colonists but sickness caused the new settlers to abandon the project and the French King re-annexed the island after the Treaty of Breda in 1667.

During the Seven Years' War, Admiral Rodney and General Monckton captured St Lucia for the English, but the island was restored to France by the Peace of Paris in 1763.

During the war of American Independence the British recaptured St Lucia, but by the Treaty of Versailles in 1783 the island was restored to the French. The island changed hands again during the war against revolutionary France, but at the Peace of Amiens in 1802 the English once again had to restore St Lucia to France. On the renewal of hostilities in 1803 the British again sought to regain St Lucia. This was accomplished on 22 June, 1803, while the French General Nogues surrendered St Lucia to British troops under Lieutenant-General Grinfield. From then St Lucia remained in the possession of the British until it became an independent member of the Commonwealth in 1979.

Dominica was discovered by Columbus on his second voyage, on

Sunday, 3 November, 1493. The island was among those included in the grant of the Patent in 1627 to Lord Carlisle by King Charles I, but all attempts at colonisation proved unsuccessful due to the stiff opposition of the warlike Caribs who were in possession of the island.

At the Peace of Aix-la-Chapelle the English and the French agreed that Dominica should remain neutral and be left to the Caribs. During the Seven Years' War the English captured the island and at the Peace of Paris in 1763 it was formally ceded to England. In 1778 it was retaken by the French, but in 1783 it was restored to England. Dominica became independent on 3 November, 1978.

Antigua was discovered by Christopher Columbus on his second voyage in November, 1493, and named Santa Maria la Antigua after a church in Seville, Spain. The first attempt at colonisation was in 1632 when Thomas Warner sent some of the colonists from St Christopher to form a colony in the island. The colonists encountered stiff opposition from the Caribs. In 1663 King Charles II made a formal grant of the island to Lord Willoughby, who sent out a large number of colonists. The island was captured by the French in 1666. However, when the Treaty of Breda was signed in 1667, Antigua was restored to England.

It remained British until 1981 when it became a fully independent state, known as Antigua and Barbuda.

St Christopher (St Kitts) and **Nevis** were discovered by Columbus on his second voyage in November, 1493.

St Kitts was the first English colony in the West Indies. It was colonised by the great pioneer, Thomas Warner. Warner landed in St Kitts on 24 January, 1624, and was welcomed by the native Caribs with whom he had established friendly relations.

After the settlement was firmly established Warner returned to England to obtain formal recognition for planting what was really the first English colony in the West Indies. Having received this from King Charles I, who appointed him Governor of St Kitts, Nevis, Barbados, and Montserrat, Warner returned to St Kitts. On the same day that he returned a number of French colonists had also landed on the island under a French privateer, Pierre Belain, Sieur d'Esnambuc. Warner invited the French to stay and soon the French colonists had set up a thriving little colony on the island.

In 1627 the English and the French agreed to divide the island between them.

By 1666, however, the French had obtained possession of the whole island, having attacked the English with the help of the Caribs and Irish malcontents. By the Treaty of Breda in 1667 the English were restored to their part of the island. In 1690 Christopher Codrington, the Governor of the Leeward Islands, captured the French part of the island and drove out most of the French colonists, but during the War of American Independence, in January, 1782, St Kitts again fell into the hands of the French. By the Treaty of Versailles, 1783, St Kitts was restored to England. St Kitts achieved independence in 1983 within the Commonwealth.

In 1628, some English planters from St Kitts settled in Nevis. The French captured the island in 1782, but it was restored to Britain in 1783. In 1967 it achieved self-government as an Associated State of Britain, and became fully independent in 1983.

Anguilla with St Kitts and Nevis entered into an Associated Statehood relationship with Britain in 1967, with Britain responsible for defence and external relations. This was not readily accepted in Anguilla, and it was formally separated from St Kitts-Nevis in 1980.

Montserrat was discovered by Columbus on his second voyage in 1493. In 1632 Irishmen from St Christopher made a settlement in Montserrat. In 1664 it fell into the hands of the French, but was restored to the English in 1668. Again in 1782 it capitulated to the French but was restored to the English in the following year and has remained so as a Crown Colony to this day.

The British Virgin Islands were discovered by Columbus on his second voyage in 1493. In 1666 a number of English colonists settled in the Islands. They were granted a charter in 1773 under which the first House of Assembly was convened on 30 November of that year. The islands have remained in the possession of the British since their colonisation.

Guyana

Modern Guyana is made up of what were formerly the three Dutch Colonies of Demerara, Essequibo, and Berbice. As the Dutch were on the side of France during the Napoleonic wars the British attacked both the French and the Dutch colonies in the Caribbean. In April 1796, Demerara, Essequibo, and Berbice surrendered to the British Major-General Whyte. At the peace of 1802 these colonies were returned to the Dutch but in the war which followed shortly after, these colonies again surrendered to a British force under Commodore Hood and General Grinfield. They were formally ceded to Britain when peace was signed in 1814 and in 1831 they were formed into one colony of British Guiana.

The Constitution of the British colony was naturally patterned on that existing in the time of the Dutch occupation, but the British pattern was established when a change of Constitution came in 1928. This provided for a unicameral legislature, the Legislative Council consisting of the Governor as President, 10 Official, 5 Nominated, and 14 Elected members.

The Executive Council consisted of 6 Official and 5 Unofficial members.

In 1943 there was a further change in the Constitution to provide for an elected majority in the Legislative, and an unofficial majority in the Executive.

In 1950 British Guiana was granted an advanced constitution, with a bi-cameral legislature comprising the House of Assembly, a State Council, and an Executive Council.

The first general election under this New Constitution was held on a franchise of Universal Adult Suffrage on 27 April, 1953 when the People's Progressive Party captured 18 of the 24 seats for Elected members in the House of Assembly. Having a clear majority of 9 this party was thus enabled to elect all 6 of their Members from the House of Assembly to the Executive Council and thus secure all 6 Ministerial posts.

Following charges that the P.P.P. was Communist dominated and that they were trying to turn British Guiana into a Communist state, the British Government suspended the constitution after six months and relieved the 6 members of the P.P.P. of their portfolios. The Governor was given full powers to administer the colony and he did so until 1 January, 1954, when an interim government was appointed to help him administer the colony.

A Commission was later appointed to consider and recommend changes to the former Constitution. Following its report in September 1954, there was a partial return of representative government with the announcement of a new Constitution on 25 April, 1956.

The 1961 Constitution

On 26 June, 1961, Her Majesty the Queen granted a new and more advanced Constitution to British Guiana with a bi-cameral legislature comprising 13 Senators, 35 elected Members and a council of ministers with the Premier and not more than 9 other ministers.

The first election under this new Constitution was held on 21 August, 1961.

After the 1961 elections there was continual friction between the two main political parties leading to racial disturbances and violence. As a result the constitution was amended to provide for new elections on the basis of Proportional Representation in a legislative assembly comprising 53 members. The elections were held on 7 December, 1964, and resulted as follows:

People's Progressive Party	24 seats
People's National Congress	22 seats
United Force	7 seats

Dr Jagan informed the Governor that he was unable to command the support of the majority of the members. Mr Burnham on the other hand was able to tell the Governor that he had been assured of the support of the United Force members which would give him majority support and Mr D'Aguiar confirmed this. Accordingly, the Governor invited Mr Burnham to accept the appointment as Premier in place of Dr Jagan.

Dr Jagan refused to resign and it became necessary for the Queen to approve an amendment to the British Guiana Constitution giving the Governor powers to appoint and remove Premiers from office.

Independence

At the Constitutional Conference held in London in November 1965, it was agreed that British Guiana should become independent under the name of Guyana. This conference was attended by representatives of the People's National Congress and United Force parties, led by the Premier, Mr Forbes Burnham, and Mr D'Aguiar respectively.

On 26 May, 1966, Guyana became independent as a dominion within the Commonwealth.

In 1970, Guyana became a Co-operative Republic. Mr Arthur Chung was elected as the Republic's first President.

In 1980, under a new constitution, the former Prime Minister, Forbes Burnham became President and Ptolemy Reid took over as Prime Minister.

On August 6, 1985, following the death of Forbes Burnham, Hugh Desmond Hoyte became President.

General elections were held in December 1985 and the People's National Congress was returned to office.

Belize

On his fourth voyage, in 1502, Columbus discovered the mainland of Central America, part of which later became British Honduras. From time to time small settlements were made by British sailors and adventurers who were attracted by the logwood which grew on the banks of the Hondo, the river Belize and the Bay Islands, but it is believed that the first real settlement was made in 1638. The Spaniards resented the presence of these logwood cutters and made several attempts to dislodge them from their settlements.

In 1717 the British Board of Trade asserted the right of the British to make settlements for logwood cutting.

By the Treaty of Paris in 1763, Spain was obliged to recognise the right of the Baymen of Honduras to cut logs and to form settlements. The settlers elected unpaid magistrates to govern them and the colony looked to Jamaica for administrative guidance.

In 1862 British Honduras was formally declared a British colony with a Lieutenant-Governor under the Governor of Jamaica. This arrangement came to an end in 1884 when a full Governor was appointed who did not have to look to Jamaica for instructions. Owing to financial difficulties the people of British Honduras petitioned Her Majesty Queen Victoria for Crown Colony status and this was granted in 1871.

In 1954, Universal Adult Suffrage was introduced. This enabled the people to elect representatives to sit on the Legislative Assembly which was made up of 15 members, 9 of whom were Elected, 3 Nominated and 3 *ex-officio* members presided over by a Speaker.

The 1960 Constitution led to greater independence. The Legislative Assembly was expanded to 25 members with 18 Elected members by Universal Adult Suffrage.

Full internal self-government was achieved on 1 January 1964 with a Constitution comprising of Her Majesty and a National Assembly consisting of a House of Representatives and a Senate.

Full independence only came in 1981, delays having occurred due to the territorial claims made on Belize by Guatemala. In the independence elections, the United Party, who have dominated politics in Belize for many years, remained in power and their leader the then premier George Cadle Price became Prime Minister.

THE UNITED NATIONS

The United Nations is an international organisation composed of sovereign states which have resolved to combine their efforts to accomplish the aims as set forth in the Charter of the United Nations. The main purposes of the United Nations are as follows:

(a) To maintain international peace and security.

(b) To develop friendly relations among nations based on respect for the principle of equal rights and self-determination of peoples.

(c) To promote social progress and better standards of life of all peoples by achieving international co-operation in the solution of international problems in the economic, social, cultural or humanitarian fields.

(d) To promote and encourage respect for human rights and for fundamental freedom for all without distinction as to race, sex, language, or religion.

The members of the United Nations are the peace-loving states of the world (at present 152 in number), who have signed the Charter, and have pledged to fulfil in good faith the obligations assumed by them in accordance with the Charter.

All member-states are sovereign, that is to say, whether they are large or small, each stands on the basis of complete equality with the other.

All members pledge to settle their international disputes by peaceful means and without recourse to armed force, to give every assistance to the United Nations in accordance with the Charter, and to refrain from giving any assistance to a state against which the United Nations is taking action.

The Charter of the United Nations was signed by representatives of

50 nations assembled at San Francisco, California, on 26 June, 1945.

The Charter of the United Nations sets out the Constitution governing the United Nations Organisation, and provides for six principal organs, namely, the General Assembly, the Security Council, the Economic and Social Council, the Trusteeship Council, the International Court of Justice, and the Secretariat.

The General Assembly consists of all the members of the United Nations, each member being represented by not more than five delegates. It meets in regular annual sessions, or more frequently as occasions may require, to discuss on any question or on any matters within the scope of the United Nations Charter, and to make recommendations to the members of the United Nations or to the Security Council or to both on any questions or matters. The General Assembly also receives and considers annual and special reports from the Security Council and from the other organs of the UN; it considers and approves the budget of the organisation and its specialised agencies, and apportions the expenses to be borne by the several members for the upkeep of the United Nations Organisations.

On the principle of the sovereign equality of all states each member of the General Assembly has one vote. The Assembly elects its President for each session. Ordinary decisions of the Assembly are taken on a majority vote of the members present and voting, but on important questions a two-thirds majority of all the members present and voting is required.

The Security Council consists of 15 members of the United Nations each having one representative. The five major powers—The United States, Russia, Great Britain, China, and France—are permanent members of this Council. The other ten members are non-permanent members and are elected by the General Assembly from among the other members of the United Nations. The non-permanent members serve for a term of two years.

The Security Council, acting on behalf of the United Nations, is primarily responsible for the maintenance of international peace and security. Each member of the Security Council has one vote.

Decisions of the Security Council on matters of procedure are taken on the affirmative votes of any 9 members. On all other matters, however, the 9 affirmative votes must include those of the 5 permanent members. Thus any one of the five permanent powers by voting against a motion for which the others have voted affirmatively can "veto" a decision of the Security Council.

The Security Council is in continuous session and the members must at all times be at the seat of the organisation.

As regards disputes which are a threat to international peace and security the Charter advises the disputants, first of all, to seek a solution by peaceful means. When necessary the Security Council will call upon the parties to settle their disputes by peaceful means and may even suggest methods of adjustment. If the parties fail to settle the dispute by peaceful means they are required to refer it to the Security Council which will then examine the pros and cons of the dispute and take effective measures to check its continuance, resorting to armed force if necessary. The decisions of the Security Council are binding upon all members who must act in accordance with their recommendations and give every assistance possible for the enforcement of the line of action decided upon by the Security Council.

The Economic and Social Council consists of 54 members of the United Nations elected by the General Assembly.

This Council deals with all international economic, social, cultural, educational, health, and related matters. It may take recommendations for promoting respect for, and observance of, human rights and fundamental freedoms for all. It co-ordinates the activities of the specialised agencies attached to the United Nations.

The Trusteeship Council deals mainly with matters connected with the mandated territories formerly administered by the League of Nations. It has limited powers.

The International Court of Justice is the principal judicial organ of the United Nations. Each Member of the United Nations has pledged to comply with the decision of the International Court of Justice in any case to which it is a party. The Court is sometimes requested to give advisory legal opinions to the Security Council and other specialised agencies of the United Nations.

The Secretariat comprises the Secretary-General and the staff of international civil servants. The Secretary-General is appointed by the General Assembly upon the recommendation of the Security Council. He is chief administrative officer of the Organisation, and acts as Secretary to the General Assembly, the Security Council, the Economic and Social Council, and the Trusteeship Council. The staff is recruited on as wide a geographical basis as possible, but the paramount consideration in their employment and conditions of service is the necessity of securing the highest standards of efficiency, competence and integrity. The Secretariat is the servant of the various organisations of the United Nations.

The seat of the United Nations is in New York.

THE UNIVERSITY OF THE WEST INDIES

The University of the West Indies is supported by and serves the following different territories in the West Indies: Antigua, Bahamas, Barbados, Belize, British Virgin Islands, Cayman Islands, Dominica, Grenada, Jamaica, Montserrat, St. Kitts-Nevis-Anguilla, St. Lucia, St. Vincent, Trinidad and Tobago. In addition, Guyana is a full participant in the Faculty of Law, and by agreement has a limited number of students in the professional faculties.

There are three campuses of the University of the West Indies—at Mona in Jamaica, at St. Augustine in Trinidad and at Cave Hill in Barbados.

At Mona are situated the Faculties of Arts and General Studies, Natural Sciences, Medical Sciences, Social Sciences and·the Faculty of Education. Students read for Special Degrees, Diplomas and Certificates offered by those Faculties and for the First Year Course only of the LL.B degree offered by the Faculty of Law.

On the Campus at St. Augustine are the Faculties of Agriculture (formerly the Imperial College of Tropical Agriculture), Engineering, Arts and General Studies, Medical Sciences, Natural Sciences, Social Sciences and Education.

The University in 1963 established its third campus in Cave Hill, Barbados, with the aid of funds for capital expenditure supplied by the British Government. At Cave Hill, students read for degrees in Arts and General Studies, Medical Sciences, Natural Sciences, Social Sciences and LL.B degrees. The Faculty of Law in which teaching began in 1970 is situated here but first year courses are also offered at the Mona and St. Augustine campuses as well as at the University of Guyana.

Enrolment (1989) stood at 11,151 students, with 5,235 at Mona, 3,882 at St. Augustine and Cave Hill.

The year 1989 also saw the commencement of teaching in Medicine, Dentistry and Veterinary Medicine at the Eric Williams Medical Sciences Complex (Trinidad).